The Book and the Body

EDITED BY

Dolores Warwick Frese
Katherine O'Brien O'Keeffe

University of Notre Dame Press
NOTRE DAME AND LONDON

© 1997 by
University of Notre Dame Press
Notre Dame, Indiana 46556
All Rights Reserved

Manufactured in the United States of America

Book design by Wendy McMillen
Set in 11/14 Joanna by Books International
Printed and bound by McNaughton & Gunn, Inc.

The author and the publisher acknowledge permission to
quote, in the essay "Getting Medieval: Pulp Fiction, Gawain,
Foucault," by Carolyn Dinshaw, from PULP FICTION: A
Quentin Tarantino Screenplay. Copyright © 1994, Quentin
Tarantino. Reprinted with permission by Hyperion.

Library of Congress Cataloging-in-Publication Data

The book and the body / edited by Dolores Warwick Frese
and Katherine O'Brien O'Keeffe
        p.   cm. — (University of Notre Dame Ward-Phillips
lectures in English language and literature; 14.)
        Includes bibliographical references (p.   ) and index.
        ISBN 0-268-00699-7 (alk. paper). —ISBN 0-268-00700-4
(alk. paper)
        1. English literature—Middle English, 1100–1500—
Criticism, Textual.   2. Christian literature, Latin (Medieval and
modern)—Criticism, Textual.   3. Learning and scholarship—
History—Medieval, 500–1500.   4. Civilization, Medieval,
in literature.   5. England—Intellectual life—1066–1485.
6. Books and reading—England—History.   7. Books and
reading in literature.   8. Manuscripts, Medieval—England.
9. Body, Human, in literature.   10. Intertextuality.   I. Frese,
Dolores Warwick.   II. O'Keeffe, Katherine O'Brien.   III. Series:
Ward-Phillips lectures in English language and literature; 14.
PR275.T45B66   1997
820.9'001—dc20   96-30288
                                                                                    CIP

∞ The paper used in this publication meets the minimum
requirements of the American National Standard for Information
Sciences—Permanence of Paper for Printed Library Materials,
ANSI z39.48-1984

Contents

Illustrations

Introduction

In *Peristephanon* 3, the twelve-year-old virgin Eulalia, "panting for God" ("anhela deo"), invites her martyrdom by kicking over the pagan images ("simulacra") she is being pressed to venerate. Immediately, as two torturers begin slicing her flesh to the bone, the late fourth-century poet Prudentius has Eulalia number her wounds:

> Scriberis ecce mihi, domine.
> Quam iuuat hos apices legere,
> qui tua, Christe, tropaea notant.
> Nomen et ipsa sacrum loquitur
> purpura sanguinis eliciti.[1]

> [Look, Lord, you are written on me. How pleasing it is to read these letters which record your triumphs, O Christ! And the purple of the drawn blood speaks your holy name.]

Before her torture, Eulalia dismissed her intact body as "limbs fashioned of clay" ("membra coacta luto"); now, however, through the praetor's forensic exactments, her body acquires a new coherence and a higher meaning. As the torturers open her body to Eulalia's gaze, she re-reads herself as a text of Christ, playing on the double significance of *scribere* to mean both 'incise' and 'write'. Her clay is "incised" producing a page that "speaks" a name in purple (imperial ink and martyrial blood). As startling as the economy of "scriberis . . . mihi" is here, Prudentius elsewhere fashions another image that focuses our attention on book and body. In his lengthy tenth poem, Prudentius records the *dicta* of Romanus, a deacon of Caesarea, who miraculously continued to declaim the errors of paganism despite having had his tongue cut out. The exactments of his martyrdom rival the tortures of the regicide Damiens, though Romanus exceeds him in cooperating with his tormentors.[2] Early and late, Romanus assists the torturers in their work of transformation (72–75; 801–10; 896–910). Like Eulalia, Romanus perceives his body as a field of discourse speaking in counterpoint to the words of his mouth. However his transitory body is to be read on earth, during his passion he is *copied* in order to be fixed in eternal memory and unchanging meaning:

> Excepit adstans angelus coram deo
> et quae locutus martyr et quae pertulit;
> nec verba solum disserentis condidit,
> sed ipsa pingens uulnera expressit stilo
> laterum genarum pectorisque et faucium.
>
> Omnis notata est sanguinis dimensio,
> ut quamque plagam sulcus exarauerit,
> altam petentem proximam longam breuem,
> quae uis doloris quiue segmenti modus;
> guttam cruroris ille nullam perdidit.
>
> (10.1121–30)

[An angel standing in the presence of God received both what the martyr said and what he

endured; he did not write down the words of
[the martyr's] discourse alone, but tracing with
his pen he portrayed the very wounds of his
sides, breast, cheeks, and jaws. Every drop of
his blood was written down, how the furrow
ploughed every wound, deep, searching, near,
long, or short; the force of the pain, the manner
of each cut; he did not waste a speck of blood.]

Though the exemplar Romanus may be hopelessly torn, the celestial copy, from the tracing of the wounds to the recording of the blood, is triumphantly exact.

In his magisterial study *European Literature and the Latin Middle Ages*, Ernst Robert Curtius cites in passing these two moments in Prudentius's celebration of martyrdom as part of his consideration of the metaphorics of the book in the early Middle Ages.[3] In a curious phrase, Curtius observes in the *Peristephanon* "many images from the book and a constant 'life relation' to it," but his further discussion neglects this hint in order to anatomize the details of the imagery of books.[4] Curtius's emphasis is on the book. But the power of Prudentius's images comes not from the book itself, but from its intersection with the bodies it informs, its "life relation[s]." While very quickly in the Middle Ages the trope of writing living words on the dead flesh of a book became a cliché, the image of writing (literally and metaphorically) on living bodies continued to have power. The book and the body are yoked by more than trope. In the years since Curtius's work, both the book and the body have seen remarkable surges in study. Work on literacy, memory, the psychology of writing, and manuscript communities reminds us that the book is a historical object and that our own literacy is a historical condition.[5] Theorizing of the body, moving from the groundbreaking work of Michel Foucault, has shown how mistaken (and how dangerous) it is to believe that the body, in its mute resistance, is beyond interpretation.[6]

The Book and the Body incorporates four essays originally presented as the 1995 Ward-Phillips Lectures at the University of Notre Dame. Their common goal was to explore the liminal areas between the book and the body as these impinge on interpretative strategies for studying material and textual corporeality in medieval England. While the approaches of these essays are various (as even a cursory glance will testify), three concerns figure and refigure themselves throughout the book: the gendered body and the copied book as sites of pain, pleasure, and desire. Memory, nostalgia, longing, and shame combine and recombine as objects of study in the essays that follow.

Mary Carruthers's essay, "Reading with Attitude, Remembering the Book," examines the medieval understanding of memory and its construction of the human body essentially as a book. The training of memory required bodily affliction, since trauma (either as bodily or mental pain) was understood to ingrain the material to be remembered in the mind. Such affliction, figured as anxiety or vexation, made the body quite literally the site for memory. The body of the boy marked by his master's birch and the surface of the parchment pricked and incised for writing share more than a common metaphor of the violence of writing. The wounding of the page and of the memory that Carruthers discusses are indeed symbiotic. In her examination of sites for memory, that is, the patternings by which information might be reliably stored and retrieved, Carruthers shows how monastic meditative exercise had as its goal the incising of patterns on the brain. "Incision," here too is more than metaphor, as current researches into neurophysiology have demonstrated. Pain in memory work was not limited to the process of learning, that is, was not only part of the procedures through which the body was marked to remember. Pain was also the trigger for the use of memory, and Carruthers shows how texts committed to memory were "vivified" through emotional suffering. Intensely affective meditation made it possible for the monk to move from "site" to "site" constructing texts from the material he had made part of his body.

Carruthers's approach to the intersections of book and body reminds us that the violence of writing (where surfaces are pounded, scraped, pierced, etched, and bound to contain thoughts as texts) is not limited to the book; that trauma, certainly productive of intense accidental memories, was programmatically used to produce stable memories in textualized bodies.

If Carruthers's essay focuses on pain to negotiate between the two objects of our thought, Michael Camille's essay looks to desire. In "The Book as Flesh and Fetish in Richard de Bury's *Philobiblon*" Camille inverts the common relationship between book and body (where the body as an instrument of memory is figured as a book) and examines, instead, the book as an object of desire. In his approach to the *Philobiblon* he employs the notion of fetish (the eroticized substitute object which provokes desire) to explore how the book as an object might become a site of subjectivity in the fourteenth century. Once again we must recall the ways in which the medieval use of the book was corporeal and its experience sensuous, quite apart from issues of aesthetics. Hair and flesh sides of folios had distinct feels, readers subvocalized, wrote in margins or interlinearly, sometimes writing glosses in dry-point (a process which incised almost invisible words in the flesh of the book). Reading was, in short, a bodily performance. It is against this background that Camille reads de Bury's treatise on his beloved books. De Bury's is a carefully coded expression of passion for the book, or, more properly, for having and holding vast numbers of them. But while the language of possession suffuses de Bury's treatise, it is also marked by an evasion of materiality at the very moment of embracing it. Quite clearly, books are less for use than for possession, and the thought that a careless reader with a dripping nose might stain his book enrages him. Camille explores the consequences of de Bury's gendering of books. Indeed, while the bibliophile in him gazes longingly on the feminized objects composing his library, the bodies of actual women are dangerous and deferred with the standard tropes of medieval misogyny. Generation takes place, nonetheless, in the library as scribes father texts. Whatever pain arose from de Bury's unsatisfiable desire for books, it is clear that towards the end of his life he knew considerable physical suffering. This too he transfers to the books who themselves complain in the treatise that they are disfigured by various bodily ills.

While Carruthers pursues the vitally embodied technologies of monastically fostered remembering and Camille the flesh and fell realities of the manuscript as fetishized maternal recollection, Seth Lerer examines the construction of the body in the Tudor court. In "The Courtly Body in Late Medieval Literary Culture," Lerer assesses the early Tudor reception of late medieval culture in order to argue for the emergence of a specifically patriarchal poetics. This legacy, whose Chaucerian patrimony involves a distinct metaphorics of corporeal display, persistently incorporates the poet's physical remains under the twin tropes of corpus-as-body and corpus-as-books. In Stephen Hawes's *Pastime of Pleasure*, the movement from manuscript to print culture is emblematized by an epitaphic sensibility featuring the authorial portrait, and the envisioning of the poet's tomb. Lerer's argument concerning such corporealization of the literary past and Hawes's repeated linkage to such tropes of embodiment are grounded in his service as a courtier of the privy chamber: poetic service is inextricably connected to the service of the royal body. Negotiating these delicate calibrations of private and public service, Lerer argues, energizes one of Hawes's major themes: the poet in exile. The spying, dissimulation, and pragmatics rehearsed in later Tudor poetry, Lerer shows, were organized earlier in the post-Chaucerian model of Pandarus. And the Criseydean dreams of dismemberment and mutilation in Hawes's *Conforte of Louers* emerge as fears of castration and rape, threats to bodily integrity—politicized as well as eroticized—which have been displaced onto Hawes's narrative self.

Similarly, in his reading of the Chaucerian *blazon anatomique*, Lerer's transposition of this literary technique to the Henrician court displays ways in which the female body, made consubstantial with the body of writing, provides the paradigm for what might be thought of as the blazonry of textual body parts. But in a complementary maneuvre, Humphrey Wellys constructs an anti-blazon through the poetic fiction of an intercepted woman's letter addressed to another woman. This letter, filled with sexual and scatological body references to the male body, vulgarizes the purported female author, indicting women in the process. Lerer goes on to show varied ways in which the privatization of Tudor reading, the inwardness generated by such praxis, and the anthologic construction of the courtly body through such figurations of the literary past subsequently occupied Wellys as he cobbled centos out of Hawes's *Pastime of Pleasure* and *Conforte of Louers*. The construction of the body of reading, and of the body of the reader as nostalgic *isolato*, are finally projected into a cento of borrowed stanzas where descriptions of the lady's body, organized into a trajectory of amatory gazing, becomes the textualized object of authorial "cutting." Lerer shows how courtly "pitee" becomes the petition on behalf of the author's book rather than the lover's body. Wellys's transformation of the Garter motto at the end of his voyeuristic performance—"Si troue Soit hony Soit qui mal y pense" [If this is discovered, evil to him who evil thinks]—thematizes the distillation of shame and the anxieties surrounding the display of courtly bodies that are Lerer's objects of attention.

Of course, the Garter motto redeployed by Wellys appears more famously at the end of the unique manuscript of *Sir Gawain and the Green Knight*. Gawain, upon his return to Camelot, displays on his naked neck the mark he has earned for his "vnleuté" (disloyalty) to Bertilak. For Gawain, the mark is a sign of his shame, but Arthur, by replicating the green "bauderyk" for all the brotherhood of his court, diffuses the shame and reinterprets it as a "swete" sign of courtly status. The text, at this moment, points to Gawain's shame and guilt only to reconfigure these as signs of comfort and fellowship. Reading against the grain in "Getting Medieval: *Pulp Fiction*, Gawain, Foucault," Carolyn Dinshaw anatomizes *SGGK* as part of her larger project to critique the Western normativity of heterosexuality even as she interrogates it. Refusing to allow the present to colonize the past, Dinshaw juxtaposes Quentin Tarantino's popular film *Pulp Fiction* and the medieval romance to show their shared agenda in abjecting the possibility of homoerotic relations between men. Foucault's *History of Sexuality*, particularly his reconstruction of sexuality in the Middle Ages, bridges the gap between these two romance texts, but Dinshaw interrogates Foucault even as she invokes him. Dinshaw tropes on a fugitive phrase in the movie where, in the aftermath of a sado-masochistic rape, the male victim announces his revenge: "I'm gonna git Medieval on your ass."

For Dinshaw, Tarantino's construction of the Middle Ages becomes the place of abjection, to which the sexually, racially, and culturally marginalized are assigned. But of all of these, what is particularly stigmatized in *Pulp Fiction* is sodomy, with anus surveillance as its mode of control. When she moves to its partner romance, *SGGK*, Dinshaw uncovers the secret scandal of the text: the contractual possibility of sex between men suggested by the narrative logic of exchange—Gawain's kiss for the Host's meat—is literally unthinkable in the text's heteronormative project of bodily construction. This, according to Dinshaw, dictates Gawain's refusal of the woman's overtures in the boudoir, since consummation there would require consummation elsewhere. In arguing for a sexually reconfigured future, whose liberated possibilities she sees thematized in the the medieval and modern romances only to be dismissed, Dinshaw adopts Foucault's (and others') project to separate acts from identities, pressing for a strategic shattering of the modern liberal subject in order to open the way for the fictioning of a future sexual politics. In the process, Dinshaw draws on her expertise as a medievalist to critique the nostalgic and often erroneous notions underlying Foucault's Middle Ages.

The 1995 Ward-Phillips Lectures "The Book and the Body" and the present volume would not have been possible without the kind support of a number of institutions and individuals at the University of Notre Dame. It is a great pleasure to acknowledge the assistance of the Paul M. and Barbara Henkels Visiting Scholars Series, whose generous grant underwrote the lecture series. Christopher B. Fox, Chair of the Department of English, and John Van Engen, Director of the Medieval Institute, gave much-needed and welcome encouragement—moral, intellectual, and financial. We should also like to record our thanks to the four contributors to this volume: Mary Carruthers, Michael Camille, Carolyn Dinshaw, and Seth Lerer both for their stimulating lectures and for their cordial cooperation in giving body to the ideas of their talks, making possible, finally, this book.

Notes

1. Aurelius Prudentius Clemens, *Carmina*, ed. Maurice P. Cunningham, Corpus Christianorum, Series Latina 126 (Turnhout: Brepols, 1966), lines 136–40. The present translations are by Katherine O'Brien O'Keeffe.

2. Michel Foucault, *Discipline and Punish: The Birth of the Prison*, trans. Alan Sheridan (New York: Random House, 1977).

3. Ernst Robert Curtius, *European Literature and the Latin Middle Ages*, trans. Willard R. Trask, Bollingen Series 36 (Princeton: Princeton University Press, 1953), 311–12.

4. Curtius, *European Literature*, 311.

5. See, for example: Janet Coleman, *Medieval Readers and Writers 1350–1400* (New York: Columbia University Press, 1981); Jacques Der-

rida, *Of Grammatology*, trans. Gayatri Chakravorty Spivak (Baltimore: Johns Hopkins University Press, 1976); Jack Goody, *The Interface Between the Written and the Oral* (Cambridge: Cambridge University Press, 1987); Eric A. Havelock, *Preface to Plato* (Cambridge, MA: Harvard University Press, 1963); Walter Ong, *Orality and Literacy: The Technologizing of the Word* (London: Methuen, 1982); Sylvia Scribner and Michael Cole, *The Psychology of Literacy* (Cambridge, MA: Harvard University Press, 1981); Brian Stock, *The Implications of Literacy: Written Language and Models of Interpretation in the Eleventh and Twelfth Centuries* (Princeton: Princeton University Press, 1983).

6. See, for example: Sarah Beckwith, *Christ's Body: Identity, Culture, and Society in Late Medieval Writings* (New York: Routledge, 1993); Peter Brown, *The Body and Society: Men, Women, and Sexual Renunciation in Early Christianity* (New York: Columbia University Press, 1988); E. Jane Burns, *Bodytalk: When Women Speak in Old French Literature* (Philadelphia: University of Pennsylvania Press, 1993); Judith Butler, *Bodies That Matter: On the Discursive Limits of "Sex"* (New York: Routledge, 1993); Joan Cadden, *Meanings of Sex Difference in the Middle Ages: Medicine, Science, and Culture* (Cambridge: Cambridge University Press, 1993); Sarah Kay and Miri Rubin, eds., *Framing Medieval Bodies* (Manchester: Manchester University Press, 1994); Linda Lomperis and Sarah Stanbury, eds., *Feminist Approaches to the Body in Medieval Literature* (Philadelphia: University of Pennsylvania Press, 1993).

THE BOOK
AND THE
BODY

CHAPTER ONE

Reading with Attitude, Remembering the Book

Mary Carruthers

This essay is not about the book as a body (even as "a body of work"), but rather about the human body as itself a sort of book, or rather, as a support for cognitive memory-work, for, as I have argued at length elsewhere, I believe that books both in antiquity and during the Middle Ages were understood primarily to be supports for human recollective work, what Latin speakers of the time called, quite indiscriminately, *memoria*.[1]

I want to begin with a work from the last third of the twelfth century, written by a Benedictine monk and contemplative, whose audience included those professional contemplatives and masters of memory-work, the Cistercians, as well as his own fellow Benedictines. This work is "On Affliction and Reading"; it is by Peter of Celle, a friend of both Richard and John of Salisbury, who, having been Abbot of the monastery of Celle in northern France, succeeded John of Salisbury as bishop of Chartres, where he died in February, 1182.[2] The title of Peter's text has long proven intriguing, being something of an oxymoron for many modern readers, and that is why I have found it a useful place to begin inventing my own meditation on bodily affliction— vexation, anxiety—as one of our primary memory tools, even for activities we tend to consider entirely "mental" or spiritual.

1

To get at this idea in terms that respect its genesis in rhetoric, I want to focus first on a trope that brings together, as a rhetorical "common place," the physiology of *memoria* and its requirement of strong emotion. This trope clusters on the Latin root, *pungo, punctus*, literally meaning to pierce, puncture, and thus wound some surface. The word quickly came as well to mean emotional vexation, anxiety, grief, and so on, and its close relative, *compunctus*, had much the same range of meanings, both the sense of piercing a surface and the emotional sense, of goading and vexing the feelings. In medieval Latin, *punctus* came to be used also as the word for the dot or pin-prick that helped to mark up a written text, and so to "punctuate" it, in our modern sense. The earliest citations given in the *Oxford English Dictionary*, from the sixteenth and seventeenth centuries, use "punctuation" particularly in the context of religious meditation and liturgical song texts, such as the Psalms: it is the method of marking up units of text into mnemonically useful length by means of "pointing" them.[3]

So we have here a chain (*catena*), mnemonically associated through the key syllable *punct-*, which attaches physical puncture-wounding, with (page) punctuation, with affective "compunction" of heart, and so from "heart" to "memory." "Heart" is a commonplace synonym for "memory" from antiquity onwards. Varro derived Latin "recordari" from "cor, cordis," an etymology preserved in our modern English idiom, "to learn by heart," meaning "to remember."[4] While I concede that sometimes a heart is just a heart, in medieval texts—especially in devotional texts—when one encounters the word *cor, cordis* it usually refers to what we call "remembering," though of an affective and recreative sort.

The "wounding" of page (in punctuation) and the wounding of memory (in "compunctio cordis") are symbiotic processes, each a requirement for human cognition to occur at all. Several scholars working on *memoria* in medieval culture, among them

Eugene Vance, Louise Fradenburg, and Jody Enders, have noted how violence seems to be a recurring preoccupation, almost a mnemotechnical principle.[5] Certainly memory writers who knew the precepts of the memory art described in the Roman Republican textbook, *Rhetorica ad Herennium*, all emphasize that making "excessive" images for secure remembering (on the observation that we recall what is unusual more readily and precisely than what is common) includes making very bloody, gory, violent "imagines agentes."

I am well aware that current psychoanalytical theory has emphasized the role of trauma in memory-making. I do not wish to be thought to believe that analysis based on these psychoanalytic constructs has no role to play in our perception of medieval cultures. But the medievals did not construct their social selves in this way, and I have noticed that scholars who use psychoanalytic language to talk about the importance of "trauma" in the undoubtedly violent lives of medieval people can neglect the more social, rhetorical roles such violence played, both in their art and their pedagogy. So instead of dealing in general with ideas of mayhem and psychic trauma, I want to concentrate quite specifically on puncture-wounds as a rhetorical figure.

I also want to talk about cognition and learning, not neurosis, for the *trope* of violence in memory-work plays a specifically mnemotechnical role. One sees its mnemonic use not only in the cultivation of anxiety-provoking images but in the actual, pervasive brutality of ancient and medieval elementary pedagogy, precisely the time in a child's life at which the most important foundational memory-work was being done. One can speak of this violence as a neurosis of medieval pedagogy: perhaps it is, but many medieval people clearly saw it as necessary to impress memories upon the brain, those all-important, rote-retained "habits" of their culture.[6]

One of the master tropes of *memoria* is that memory is like a waxed tablet, or later in manuscript cultures, like the page of a parchment—upon which we each individually write with the "stylus" or "pen" of our memory. I have described this model and some of its implications at length in The Book of Memory: one finds it as early as Homer, certainly in Plato, the Book of Proverbs, Cicero, Quintilian, Augustine, Jerome, and then down through the ages. Now this model of memory is essentially a locational one: matters are written into a "place" in memory as characters are impressed into a tablet or incised onto parchment. The physical book's surfaces provide "support" for the laid-out page, including its decoration and punctuation, and these features in turn "support" the memory of a reader by providing visual cues to the "matters" of a work (visual cues in the form of written letters, dots and curlicues, pictorial images, and all that) that can be "placed" away in memory.

I think most modern scholars, contemplating this image of memory as a written tablet, are inclined to imagine it much too statically and indolently. I would like to focus on the vigorous, if not actually violent, activity involved in making a mark upon such a physical surface as an animal's skin. You must break it, rough it up, "wound" it in some way with a sharply pointed in-strument. Erasure involved roughing the physical surface up even more: medieval scribes, erasing parchment, had to use scrapers. In other words, writing was always hard physical labor, very hard as well on the surface on which it was being done; this vigorous physical aspect, I believe, was always part of that master model of memory as a written surface.

For example, there is a well-known manifestation of this trope, popular in later medieval piety, that likens the body of Christ to a written parchment page. One especially gory version of it is an English poem from the fifteenth century, the so-called "Long Charter" of Christ. The author of this poem calls his image a "memoria" and also a "pictura," both designed for meditation. Christ is imagined to speak from the cross. He likens himself to a piece of vellum, stretched out "as parchment ought to be." The blood which runs from his wounds is the ink (both red and black) which we "see" on the page, and the scourges and thorns of his torture are the pens which incised those inked letters onto the surface.[7]

Classical pedagogy, inherited by the early Middle Ages through the practices of the monasteries, was a memory-based pedagogy, formed especially on teaching reading through memory work, meditation. The many memory exercises were like physical exercises, designed, in Galen's phrase, as a "gymnastic of the soul." The idea was that rhetorical training was a kind of military training.[8] Thus there was always a military cast to the model both of rhetorical education and the office of an orator in civil life: one need search no further than Cicero for splendid examples of this. These connections carry over into monastic meditation. Peter of Celle sees the connection of affliction and reading primarily in military terms:

> newly enlisted soldiers of Christ, who fight under the banner of the cross, are subjected to a strenuous, three-fold test: bodily affliction by which the body's wantonness is curbed; reading of the Old and New Testaments, by which the soul is fed; prayer of compunction for sins . . . which raises the spirit to God.[9]

The military image of the monk, often attached (and rightly so) to Old Testament and Pauline sources, incorporates as well I believe this common Roman model of the orator, especially the forensic orator. Cicero's rhetor is a warrior, doing battle against the (false) persuasions of the community's enemies. He employs the matters of his memory, the texts and stories and images, to do battle against the enemies of the common good. To find such a model of reading in the rhetoric of monasticism, one need look no further than Benedict's Rule: "[W]e must prepare our hearts and our bodies to do battle under the holy obedience of His commands. . . . And so [notice the causal connection] we are going to establish a study-center. . . ."[10] Cenobitic monasticism from the beginning thought of itself as a city—a city protected and sustained by its own kind of civic oratory, derived, in this case, from Scripture.[11]

In this city or citadel (and remember that the two things are identical in cultures that built walled cities) the soldier-monk-orator uses his memory as his weaponry. The action of reading becomes a kind of battlefield of virtue and vice. Here again is Peter of Celle:

> One who does not devote himself to holy reading disarms his ramparts of a thousand shields which might hang down from them. How quickly and easily is the city of one's room captured if one does not now defend oneself with God's help and the shield of the sacred page? . . . Take projectiles from your bookcase so that when you are struck you may strike back at the one who struck you and force him to speak.[12]

These images of the "citadel," of "the little city of your cell," of the "bookcase" in which are stored the weapons with which to defend yourself have much resonance in mnemonic technique. Even language which we may not recognize as metaphorical is: the Benedictine and Cistercian monks of Peter's audience did not actually have "bookcases" in their "cells": the monastery *armaria* were usually in the cloister, and the monks did not usually have private cells. So the "bookcase" in "your cell" should be understood in a mostly figurative way, as the monk's memory-cell, in which the texts he has armed himself with are kept ready to hand (or rather "to memory").[13]

The brain is not just a single parchment but a whole library of books. These materials are cut (incised) into the brain, as units of text and image like the bits of punctuated text on a book page. They are "projectiles," in Peter's arsenal—weapons like spears and javelins that make puncture wounds, or "puncti," the units also of punctuation, and they are incised in memory and brought forth through com-punc-tion or anxious care—that is, "affliction."

Such connections are inherent in the verb "meditate" itself. The Latin *meditare* is used to translate the Greek verb *meletein* in many fourth and fifth century ascetic texts. *Meletein* meant to perform exercises, both physical exercises as soldiers do, and also the memory exercises associated with learning to read and write.[14] It was quickly extended to the memory exercises associated with learning to read and write, but which continued throughout a young man's schooling. Such exercises were thought to shape the brain, as a gardener prunes trees or a sculptor cuts away stone or a scribe incises parchment (all of these are commonplace tropes for the process). And the agency of this shaping is memory, practicing over and over like a wheel ("rote") one's *res, dicta*, and *facta memorabilia*. But one does not practice these sporadically or one loses their good, just as one does not (even now) undertake a program of muscular exercise in a hit or miss fashion. The metaphors buried within the English word "rote" ("wheel" and "route," both from Latin *rota*) imply the orderly disposition of the various "bits" of memory: the "things" of a culture are learned within repeated, patterned sequences, the "little forms" or *formulae*—a bit of text and/or a picture—with which meditation began. These provide the structured/structuring "backgrounds" or "places," the "habits" (as in "habitation") of one's own thinking mind. Notice the crucial locational emphasis that underlies these common concepts.[15] Memory-places are not significant as "ideas" themselves, but as the forms or molds upon which, out of other pieces of memory, ideas are constructed. They tell us *where* we are. This is not a content-bearing or informational function, but an inventive function: they give us "attitude." Or in other words, you cannot "read" (I use the word loosely) without first finding your "place," without locating yourself physically, emotionally, within and towards what you are reading, whether that is a book or a program of sculpture or a whole cathedral. You must always first find out where you stand.

This makes the task of reading first and foremost into a locational one, and thus into a problem both of memory and of invention. But the notions of what constitutes "memory" and "invention" have changed significantly from the pre-modern centuries of the West to the rationalist individualism of the nineteenth century. Most importantly, both "invention" and "memory" in antiquity and through the Middle Ages had their most extensive attention and practice in the domain of rhetoric, rather than psychology or what we now call the "philosophy of mind." We should not forget this critical difference from our own intellectual habits. We tend now to think of rhetoric primarily as persuasion of another, distinguishing "rhetoric" from "self expression" (a distinction now often built into the syllabi of American college composition courses). But ancient rhetoric also emphasized invention, and, in the culture that is my focus here— Western monasticism—the techniques of rhetoric became primarily focused not on tasks of public persuasion but on tasks of what is essentially literary invention.

The Latin word *inventio* gives rise to two separate words in modern English. First is our word "invention," meaning the "creation of something new" (or at least different). These creations can be either ideas or material objects, including of course works of art and literature. We also speak of people having "inventive minds," by which we mean that they have many creative ideas, and they are good at "making," to use the Middle English synonym of "composition."

The other modern English word derived from Latin *inventio* is "inventory." This word refers to the storage of many diverse materials, but not to random storage: clothes thrown into the bottom of a closet cannot be said to be "inventoried." Inventories must have an order. Their materials are counted and placed in locations within an overall structure which allows any item to be retrieved easily and at once. This requirement also excludes inventories that are too cumbersome or too indistinguished to be cognitively useful: by all reports, much of the U.S. government's property cannot be said to be "inventoried" any more than can the contents of my handbag.

Inventio has both these meanings in Latin, and this observation points to a fundamental assumption about the nature of "creativity" in that culture. Having "inventory" is a requirement for "invention." Not only does this statement assume that one cannot create ("invent") without a memory store ("inventory") to invent from and with, but it also assumes that the memory-store is properly "inventoried," that its matters are in "locations." Some locational structure is a prerequisite for any inventive thinking at all.

These structures need not bear a relationship to the "art of memory" described in the Republican Roman Rhetorica ad Herennium, the fortunes of which was the subject of Frances Yates's pioneering work, The Art of Memory.[16] To limit the study of "locational memory" to this one variety obscures both the generic concept and the medieval and even Renaissance developments of memoria. In addition to (and more important than, at least through the thirteenth century) the precepts of the ad Herennium there developed very early on in Christianity a disciplina or via of inventive meditation on a memorized locational inventory that was called by the monks memoria spiritalis or sancta memoria. This meditative tradition also was deeply implicated in the pedagogy of ancient rhetoric, making many of the same assumptions about "invention" and how it is to be done that we find more generally in non-Christian sources. As a consequence it did not develop in total isolation from the ancient rhetorical praxis of invention and composition. The monastic art also employed a "locational memory," as its foundational schema.

Before I discuss further how invention was related to locational memory, and what both have to do with "wounding" memory, however, I need to make another elementary definition, elementary because it is not peculiar to any one mnemonic technique, but is shared by many, because these techniques build upon (or at least so it was thought) the natural requirements of human learning and thinking. First of all, human memory operates in signs, which take the form of images that call up material not immediately present to one. So in addition to being signs, all memories, even those composed of words, are also images (*phantasiai*).[17] Moreover, these images are composed of two elements: a "likeness" that serves as a cognitive cue or token to the "matter" or "res" being remembered *and* an *intentio* or emotional "gut reaction" to the remembered experience. Memories are all cognitive images, and they are all and always "colored."

A recent article in the *New York Times* about developments in neuropsychology reported that "emotional memories involving fear [other emotions seem not to have been part of the test] are permanently ingrained on the brain; they can be suppressed but never erased. . . . Researchers have come to realize that emotional brain circuits are just as tangible as circuits for seeing, hearing, and touching. . . . Emotions and feelings are not . . . ephemeral . . . [but] are largely the brain's interpretation of our visceral reaction to the world."[18] This view bears a striking relationship to the medieval one, that memory-images of whatever sort require emotional coloring to be laid down strongly for secure recovering; and that these memories exist not discretely but in "circuits" or networks.

In "On Affliction and Reading," Peter of Celle assumes that "bodily affliction" is a prerequisite of reading in order "that the body's wantonness is curbed." "Affliction" or "anxiety" for Peter of Celle is thus the opposite of "wantonness," a word which has its roots in the idea of "wandering"—again, a spatial and locational idea. "Error" is analyzed in these cultures as first a matter of pathways and networks—a cognitive matter—before it is a matter of "falsity" or "obliteration," matters of epistemology and

ontology. Peter says in particular that affliction is
"the spirit of fornication." But what does "forn⸱
do with cognitive networks?[19]

The great vice of *memoria* (both *spiritalis* ⸱
not forgetting, but disorder. This vice came to ᴜᴄ
monks *curiositas*. In terms of mnemotechnic, it constitutes ⸱
"crowding"—a mnemotechnical sin because crowding images
together blurs them and thus dissipates their effectiveness for
orienting and cuing—and also randomness, having backgrounds
without any order and thus without any "routes" (a problem
that will inevitably lead to "error," wandering about). *Curiositas* is
well described by John Cassian. The mind, Cassian says, cannot
be empty of thought. But it is inclined to laziness and a kind of
wandering that Cassian categorizes as a form of "mental fornication." He describes what is apt to happen:

> Our minds think of some passage of a psalm. But it is taken away
> from us without our noticing it, and, stupidly, unknowingly, the
> spirit slips on to some other text of Scripture. It begins to think
> about it, but before it gets fully to grasp it, another text slides into
> the memory and drives out the earlier one. . . . The spirit rolls along
> from psalm to psalm, leaps from the gospel to St. Paul, from Paul to
> the prophets, from there it is carried off to holy stories. Ever on the
> move, forever wandering, it is tossed along through all the body of
> Scripture, unable to settle on anything, unable to reject anything or
> hold on to anything, powerless to arrive at any full and judicious
> study, a dilettante and a nibbler of spiritual ideas rather than their
> creator and possessor. . . . Three things keep a wandering mind in
> place—vigils, meditation, and prayer. Constant attention to them
> and a firm concentration upon them will give stability to the soul.[20]

The root metaphors in this passage are entirely locational: "wandering" against "having a way" or "a route." Or being *mobilis* and
vaga as contrasted to having *status*, a place to stand, and so to be
stabilis.[21] Mnemotechnical *curiositas* results from sloth, laziness, a

.nd that neglects to pay attention to thinking as a process of building. One cannot build without patterns, the builder's form-making tools.

These patterns, whether of words (text) or of decoration (including punctuation of all sorts), become incised permanently in the brain like the ruts that kept wheels on the route of medieval roads. Distraction leads to "error," wandering from "the way" or mnemotechnical cognitive schemata. Either one loses one's mnemonic associations, the "matters" that the mental cues one has adopted are supposed to call up (perhaps the most common fault of novices in *memoria*), or one loses the map itself (the "locations" in their order), or one slips from one "map" (perhaps a psalm) to another one (perhaps something in the *Aeneid*) via a common cue or key-word. The remembering mind, said Geoffrey of Vinsauf, is a "cellula deliciarum," a little chamber of pleasures.[22] That is both its power and its liability, and like the rest of the physical body, it needs disciplined exercise but it also needs to have its limits respected: not to be over-worked, and to be given a suitable regimen, both of mental "matters" and of physical diet and rest.

John Cassian discusses another problem besides "crowding," one which also derives from mnemotechnical *curiositas*. It is often presented by modern historians as a problem of forgetting, but I think Cassian is really talking about a matter of mnemonic praxis rather than one of complete obliteration of memory. It is a problem that comes up with some frequency in the confessional literature of early Christians who had grown up in a traditional Roman education: the continuing mnemonic and emotional hold of the pagan literature which they had memorized by rote as children.[23]

This particular conversation is held with the Egyptian monk, Abba Nesteros, to whom the novice, Cassian, and some companions have come for training. The problem with which Nesteros has been presented by Cassian is the young man's inability to forget his classical education. "The insistence of my *paedogogus* and my own urge to read continuously have so soaked into me that at this point my mind is infected by those poetic works, tales of war in which I was steeped from the beginning of my basic studies when I was very young. . . . When I am singing the psalms or else begging pardon for my sins the shameful memory of poems slips in or the image of warring heroes turns up before my eyes." This is a case of mnemotechnical distraction, when the associational pathways "leak," as it were, from one mental network to another. Its solution is to set different "backgrounds," new structuring habits or "little forms." Nesteros counsels Cassian to "re-place" his memory network, blocking one set of locations by another: "All you need is to transfer to the reading and meditation of the spiritual writings the same care and the same attention which, you said, you had for worldly studies."[24]

This solution embodies a fundamental assumption about how humans think. First, human thinking is not a disembodied "skill"; there is no thought without matters to think with. Secondly, people can think only with the contents of their memories, their experiences. And human memories are stored as images in places. One's backgrounds are orderly and stable, once one has learned them, but the images within in them can be changed readily, depending upon the occasion. Nesteros's solution to "forgetting" is one by one to replace the "topics" in his novice's memory with a new set of "places," this time drawn from the Bible. Notice that the condition of remembering is considered to be the cognitive norm—the novice suffers from an excess of remembering. So "forgetting"—far from being natural to a human mind—requires particular acts of concentrated mnemotechnical attention, during which one "drives out" one set of memory "topics" and replaces them with another. And this is analyzed further as a problem of orienting the will, of (as Cassian says) "care and attention."

The difficulty spoken of results from the fundamentals of classical education, a set of methods that built solidly upon procedures of memory. It has often been described, though still without equal, in my opinion, in the studies of Henri Marrou; it prevailed in elementary schools in the West from antiquity through much of the nineteenth century.[25] Children were taught the foundational texts twice, once to learn by heart the sounds of the words, syllable by syllable, and then, a second time, to attach to those sounds their meaning and commentary. In this method, the phrases of the foundation text, first "divided" into "sound-bytes" (syllables, roots, and phrases of short-term memory length) and then in that form fully "digested" and made virtually a part of the child's physiological make-up by rote exercises, served as a fixed set of backgrounds to which further matters (in "images") could be attached, in the manner of basic mnemonic technique. The role of "rote learning" then—as now in Koranic, Talmudic, Vedic, and Buddhist scriptural schools—is to lay a firm foundation for all further education, not so much as "information" but as a series of mnemonically secure inventory "bins" into which additional matter could be stored and thence recovered. This explains the problem that Cassian encountered; his old backgrounds were getting in the way of his new learning.

The "worthless stories" "steeped" and "infected" and "saturated" him—notice how physiological these words are, as though the basic, rote-learned texts were a part of his very body. That in fact was the desired effect. The rote material was thought to provide the ethical templates, the predispositions and even the moods, for virtually all subsequent ethical, religious, cultural, and intellectual activity—John Cassian writes of it literally as the mind's "fodder," its "guts":

> If [your mind] . . . feeds upon [divine texts], either it will be able to
> expel its previous "topics" one at a time, or abolish them altogether.
> The human mind is unable to be empty of all thought. If it is not en-

gaged with spiritual matters it will necessarily be wrapped up in what it previously learned. As long as it has nowhere else to go while in its tireless motion, its irresistible inclination is toward matters with which it was imbued since infancy, and it mulls over incessantly those materials which long commerce and attentive meditation have given it to think with. Spiritual knowledge must therefore achieve a similarly long-lasting, secure strength in you. . . . It is something to be hidden away within you, perceived as though it were palpable, and felt in your guts. . . . If these matters, having been lovingly gathered up, hidden away, and marked for identification in a compartment of your memory, [are then called up] . . . they will pour forth like a great fragrance from the vessel of your heart. . . . And so it will happen that not only your memory's concentrated meditations but all its wanderings and strayings will turn into a holy, unceasing rumination of the Law of the Lord."[26]

Notice the assumptions that John Cassian makes here. The mind never stops thinking—it cannot be emptied of thought. A "good" memory not only is supplied with rote material, but these have been made its "places," the laid out compartments or bins of memory; the matter in each is appropriately marked out and indicated mnemonically. Whatever new is taken in and learned must be linked into this memory construction by meditation, the "rumination" of mnemotechnical murmur ("silent" reading).[27] If one has fully made such a memory, holy thoughts will "flow out from the channels of experience" (that is, the networks of a linked-up memory) and "bound forth . . . unceasing, from the bottomless ocean of your heart."[28] Even at rest, even when day-dreaming (and night-dreaming too) your mind, wheeling through the routes of its images cannot think about anything else than the Law of the Lord, because—ideally—it has nothing else to think with.

In his first conference, Cassian likens the mind thinking to a great millwheel:

This exercise of the heart [that is, meditation] is compared . . . to that of a mill which is activated by the circular motion of water. The mill cannot cease its operations at all so long as it is driven round by the pressure of the water and it, then, becomes quite feasible for the person in charge to decide whether he prefers wheat or barley or darnel to be ground. And one thing is clear. Only that will be ground which is fed in by the one who is in charge. . . . if we turn to the constant meditation on Scripture, if we lift up our memory to the things of the spirit . . . then the thoughts deriving from all this will of necessity be spiritual. . . . However, if we are overcome by sloth or by carelessness, if we give ourselves over to dangerous and useless chattering . . . there will follow in effect from this a harvest of tares to serve as a ministry of death to our hearts.[29]

Notice that Cassian places the entire ethical burden upon the "miller," the person who feeds raw material into the mill to be ground by the whirling stone. Whether it be wheat or tares is, in this model, a matter of choice, of will. "Bad" memory is the result of sloth and of distraction—that is, of "curiosity." The infantile habits, the inviscerated texts ("inviscerata" is the word Cassian uses) of childhood can, with effort, be dis-placed [*expellandum*], he says, presumably into an infrequented corridor of memory. The figure of human digestion, including excretion, that lies behind this whole discussion is evident, and deliberate.

Dis-placement is a memory technique. The twentieth-century Soviet memory-artist, Shereshevski, was the subject of a detailed case-study by the distinguished Soviet neuropsychologist, A. R. Luria, published in English as *The Mind of a Mnemonist*. Shereshevski complained of his inability to forget anything: he had to remember and recall thousands of images during his work as a vaudeville artist and eventually he became worried about overcrowding his memory. He tried many methods, including writing down some of his schemes, imagining them burning up in a fire, but only when he realized that all he needed to do was *choose to forget* them did they securely disappear. This is another instance of mnemotechnical "curiosity" (not Luria's word for it, of course) and its cure: careful, focused attention.[30]

There is another dimension to *curiositas* besides this one of the "crowding" and *confusio* of the images and *formae mentis*. This meaning of "curiositas" has to do with the mind-set (as it were) of the thinker. Being *curiosus* is the opposite of the state of being *attentus*, "attentive" and "concentrated." It is what happens when you lose track of what your images are cues for. Greek *meletein*, the verb meaning "to perform exercises," including the rote memory exercises of beginning reading, is related to the root *mele-*, meaning "attention," "care," and also "anxiety." There is a whole mnemonic chain of associations in Greek built upon the syllable *mel-*: besides *meletein* and *melete*, there are *mel-is*, "honey," *mellite*, "bee," and *mel-ine*, "a kind of grain" and the "bread" made of this grain (remember also the "mill" image used by John Cassian); there is *mel-a-*, "dark," as in "melancholy," the dark humor said to characterize people with especially creative, strong memories; there is *mel-os*, meaning "limb" and also "song" and "melody." These all yield important tropes for the operations of a trained human memory.[31] Latin also had a chain of associations that linked "anxiety" into inventive *memoria*, but by another network, deriving from the first syllable of *curiositas* (cur-). This set of puns will become clear in the final example I want to discuss of an effort to "forget" that resolves itself not as a need to obliterate but as a need to curb *curiositas* by finding one's "stable place" to attend to the wandering and wantonness of "mental fornication."[32]

In 1140 Bernard of Clairvaux composed a sermon for men who sought to enter the Cistercian order. He was addressing an already clerical audience, one seeking to become part of an elite: masters of a particularly difficult art of memory-work.[33] *Curiositas*, as we have seen, is a failure to "take care," a vice of dilettantism, when we become so charmed by the play of our mental images that we lose their "place" and cannot remember what path they were supposed to mark. The solution is not to do away with these images but to focus them and order them, either to put them into service or to will them into different, less frequented "places" altogether.

Bernard counsels the young monks about how to "forget" their memories of past, pre-claustral experience before conversion. The root metaphor of "turning" in the verb "convert" is very much a part of Bernard's play in this sermon, turning memories, turning associations—questions of use and goal that resolve themselves into questions of will. Bernard begins, memorably, with a turn on the trope of "the stomach of memory" (a subset of the memory-as-digestion trope). Quoting Jeremiah 4:19 (a conventional text in such contexts), "Ventrum meum doleo," literally "I have pains in my gut," Bernard asks rhetorically, "How can I not have pain when the gut of my memory is filled with putrid stuff?"[34] The problem, clearly, is posed as a problem of memory. And the answer lies in *conversio*, a matter of will.

It has been suggested that what Bernard wants (and what this whole monastic trope of cleansing memory, which one also finds in Cassian, intends) is the replacement of the "empirical" facts of one's past life by "ideas": "Bernard's monk seems to have trained himself to a habitual loss of self, distinguished by a purged memory and a capacity for remembering only the universal experiences of the sensual delights of Scripture."[35] But is oblivion of self what Bernard in fact counsels? Is amnesia what he means by cleansing of memory (having "memoria munda," as he calls it)?[36] In other words, is "forgetting" as Bernard understands it in this sermon really equivalent to "obliteration"?

As we have seen in the passage from John Cassian examined above, the complete obliteration of specific memories, while held out as a theoretical possibility for a master of the art, was recognized to be extremely difficult. It was also, certainly by Bernard's time, not compatible with the monastic praxis of "compunctio cordis," the beginning of prayer. Bernard says that *only our own sins* can move us to shame and contrition: we may think about those of other people but they will not *affect* us, make us *care*.[37]

Bernard addresses the problems of obliteration through another figure. He changes his governing model from that of digestive excretion [that is, *expellandum*], to that of "coloring," dyeing a fabric or writing on a parchment:

> In what way will my life be displaced from my memory? A thin, fragile parchment deeply soaks up the ink; by what craft may it be erased? For it does not take the dye just at the surface, but the skin has been colored straight through. In vain should I try to scrape it away; the parchment rips before the messy letters are erased. Amnesia could completely erase my memory, as, deranged in my mind, I should not remember the things I had done. Short of that, what scraper could bring it about that my memory would remain whole and yet its stains be dissolved? Only that living, powerful word, more cutting than any two-edged sword: "Your sins are forgiven you." . . . [God's] forgiveness blots out sin, not in causing it to be lost from my memory but in causing something which before used to be both in my mind and dyed into it by my moral habits to be still in my memory but no longer to stain it in any way. . . . Cast out guilt, cast out fear, cast out confusion, for this is what full pardon of sins brings about, in such a way that not only are they no obstacle to our salvation but cooperate in our good."[38]

The master metaphor in this passage is that of writing on parchment of wretched quality, and therefore one which takes the ink porously, leaving letters which are ragged and blotted. The only way to erase such a parchment is to destroy it altogether: the knife or scraper (or pumice stone) which medieval scribes used to efface their mistakes will only tear such fragile material.

The point of Bernard's metaphor, therefore, is that one *cannot* simply obliterate memory. Whatever you do to erase what is written there (short of killing off the parchment, as it were) will be ineffective: you will still be able to read the letters in the manuscript of your memory. So the only way to "forget" your sins is to ask God's forgiveness and then change your attitude, your "intention," towards them.

This idea derives from what was considered to be a basic fact of memory images: they are composed of both a "likeness" and an "intention," or emotional response. What forgiveness changes is the image's *intentio*, one's emotional direction, the root metaphor in *converto*, towards the memory images that still exist in one's mind, including all those personal memories that make up "my life." The key, as usual, is the moral use one makes of them: no longer producers of guilt or fear or *confusio*, they can "cooperate in our good," if we "take care" to use them well.[39]

This may be a very odd idea to us, for it assumes a degree of conscious control over one's own emotions that is quite foreign to our own psychologies, predicated as many of them are on a notion that emotion is a part of "the unconscious" and uncontrollable, except indirectly. It also couches this control in terms of "attitude," emotional "direction," even "point of view." One's *stance* towards one's memory-images is critical to their moral utility—and this fact brings us around again to the importance of *status* and *stabilis*. Notice again the fundamentally locational and visual nature of the metaphor buried in these words.

Like many vices, *curiositas*, properly balanced and moderated, can be a virtue. Peter of Celle begins his treatise "On Conscience" by observing that "the religious mind inquires with religious curiosity about religious conscience."[40] The word is related to *cura* ('care') and its classical meaning, and meaning in some verses of the Bible, is "careful." So there is both bad *curiositas* or distraction, a sort of extreme remembering (both overly much and overly little), and good *curiositas*—"carefulness," "attentive play of mind," or "being mindful." The good sort is known by its synonym, the word for it one finds in medieval mnemonic technique: *sollicitudo*.

And the control we have of *sollicitudo* hinges upon our mental habitation: location again.

From earliest Christian times, it was considered especially useful to begin prayer by focusing on images, especially the Cross, that evoked strong emotions of what came to be called "compunction." As the praxis of meditation developed, "compunctio cordis" became elaborated in a variety of "ways" to induce strong emotions of grief and/or fear, including an emotion-filled imagining as one recites or chants the Psalms, the Passion, and other suitable texts, strongly emotional reflection upon one's sins and sinful state, and the specific task of "remembering Hell" in vigorous sensual detail.

Students of religion and spirituality are very familiar with this first task of meditation. I would like to underscore here, however, some ways in which this familiar technique overlays certain technically mnemonic features. *Compunctio cordis* itself is a phrase that employs a familiar pun, "the heart" as the seat of emotional life, especially pity, and "the heart" as a standard synonym for the memory. Thus, for this culture, implied in the very word *recordari* is an act of remembering not "in tranquillity" but by means of very strong emotion.

And the emotion is initiated and called up by a useful image, a recollective cue that most often takes the form of what we would now call a picture. One places oneself in front of this picture and looks at it, thus initiating one's inventive process. For example:

> My heart considers and reconsiders what it has done and what it deserves. Let my mind descend into "the land of darkness and the shadows of death," and consider what there awaits my sinful soul. Let me look inwards and contemplate, see and be disturbed; O God, what is this that I perceive, the land of "misery and darkness"? Horror! horror! What is this I gaze upon . . . a confusion of noises, a tumult of gnashing teeth, a babble of groans. Ah, ah, too much, ah, too much woe! Sulphurous flames, flames of hell, eddying dark-

nesses, swirling with terrible sounds. Worms living in the fire . . .
devils that burn with us, raging with fire and gnashing your teeth
in madness, why are you so cruel to those who roll about among
you? . . . Is this the end, great God, prepared for fornicators and de-
spisers of your law, of whom I am one? Even I myself am one of
them! My soul, be exceedingly afraid; tremble, my mind; be torn,
my heart. . . . Good Lord, do not recall your just claims against your
sinner, but remember mercy towards your creature.[41]

This is from St. Anselm of Bec's second Meditation, an invention upon two verses from Job: "I go whence I shall not return, even to the land of shadows and shadow of death and no
order."[42] In fact this entire composition is woven from remembered texts, from Job, the Psalms, Revelations, and the Gospels
together with their accrued commentary, which included (especially by the time Anselm was writing in the mid-eleventh century) programs of meditational pictures that were part of the
interior "viewing" of Hell during prayer.

But the texts are vivified, given a cognitive energy through
Anselm's own emotions. "Rumination," a word often used for
this activity in studies of spirituality (and in discussions of
memory-work), is perhaps too peaceful and too introspective in
its modern connotations quite to suit the anguish of Anselm's
reading. He is literally getting himself all worked up. The "careful" internal viewing of these remembered texts, their syllables
allowed to "gather in" other *dicta et facta memorabilia* as Anselm's
associations collect them up, is done with as much "care," in the
emotional sense, as possible. He scares himself, he grieves himself, he shames himself: this is *com-punc-tio cordis*, wounding oneself with the text and picture. It is cued to the texts as "punctuated" in the book, both actual and that in Anselm's memory,
those clauses of text each of which is of a length of one unit of
the mind's *conspectus* or mental gaze, and inscribed and inviscer-

ated in our bodies as small puncture wounds inscribe a tattoo on skin ("tattoo" being another ancient meaning of compunctio).

I would like to close by examining a well-known bit of advice about meditational method. It is by Bruno of Querfort, a disciple of the famous eleventh-century mystic, St. Romuald of Camaldoli (d. 1027), and I would like you to notice the importance of physical location and of mental play, especially in the form of visual as well as verbal punning, in this brief excerpt:

> Sit within your cell as though in paradise; cast to the rear of your memory everything distracting, becoming alert and focused on your thoughts as a good fisherman is on the fish. One pathway [to this state] is through [reciting] the Psalms; do not dismiss this. If you cannot manage to get through them all [at one sitting] as you used to do with the fervor of a novice, take pains to chant the psalms in your spirit now [starting] from this place now from that, and to interpret them in your mind, and when you begin to wander in your reading, don't stop what you are doing, but make haste to recapture your attentiveness; place yourself [pone te] above all in the presence of God with fear and trembling, like one who stands in the gaze of the emperor; pull yourself in completely and crouch down like a baby chick, content with God's gift, for, unless its mother provides, it can neither taste nor acquire what it eats.[43]

While St. Romuald, it is true, was a hermit, whose distinctive variety of monasticism emphasized a goal of living in solitude, the word "cell" is not to be taken only literally here: indeed the passage contains several word-plays, a number of which resonate within memory technique.[44] "Sede in cella" (especially since few monks in the eleventh century had private cells) plays on the standard metaphor of memory as a room or cella, as well as a "cellar," where nourishment is stored (inventoried) in an orderly fashion (or at least it should be). A cell is a four-sided figure, or a cube, or a "central" square, a favorite shape with which to initiate meditation.

Sede plays on a common metaphor for the locations of memory, the "seats" or *sedes* in which material, such as the memorized psalms, are stored in their order. So the command, "sede in cella," is a directional one: locate yourself in a "seat" of memory "as though in paradise"—for the memory-work of heaven. A good "way" is by means of a journey through the Psalms. Notice the admonition to begin "now in this place, now in that": the individual psalms are imagined as "seats" or "places" in a journey (*via*), whose map is in your memory. Hugh of St. Victor, some hundred years later, uses virtually the same image for the *sedes* of the psalms in his mnemotechnical preface to his Chronicle.[45] The psalms, evidently for St. Romuald as for St. Benedict of Nursia before him and Hugh of St. Victor after him, are the foundation of monastic *studium* and of subsequent *memoria*; as a novice, one learned them all and could recite them straight through (or however one chose to do so). Bruno's account refers to the monastic belief that "reading," in the full sense of monastic *memoria spiritalis*, begins with getting the psalms, in their places, by rote. An older monk might not still be able to do this—but notice that St. Romuald assumed that even a tired, fading, old memory can begin reading—that is, mentally—starting "now from this place now from that." The word he uses is *locus*, and it is clear that this description assumes that his own trained, stocked, locational memory inventory is at the monk's individual disposal at all times.

You should be in a state of focused alertness, *sollicitudo*, like a fisherman watching out for fish. This is another common trope for memory-work; it has ancient antecedents, and we still "fish" for a recollection.[46] When your mind (and memory) wanders, you must call it back to attention. You do this by giving yourself an emphatic emotional jolt. In fear and trembling, you "place yourself" in imagination, in the presence and gaze of God. In other words, anxiety is a requirement of mnemonic art: it "locates" you in your reading-place.

But you do not stop with the simple emotion of fear. Notice next how Romuald (speaking through Bruno) "jump-starts" the play of his mind by an amusing and multivalent image: the scene of a baby chick (pullus) cowering fearfully under the gaze of an emperor. The imperial bird is an eagle, and (especially since you are to think of yourself as a chick) you may imagine the imperial gaze as that of an eagle contemplating its next meal: you, the chick. Visualize this to yourself. Bruno-Romuald gets to this picture via a chain of memorial associations: starting off from the technical requirement to manufacture in oneself a state of "fear and trembling" (sollicitudo, anxiety, compunctio). Anxiety takes him to emperor, from there to eagle to chick to food to God to mother. Not all these connections are explicitly made in the written text—to do so would defeat the purpose of engaging the reader. Enough are made, and the image is amusing enough, to catch our attention and to put our own minds "in play," as a "way in" to our own further creative meditation (which is the point). Such associational play is the very stuff of memoria.

But the play is set in motion and guided consciously. The emperor-eagle-chick complex is an ornament of style (the rhetorical ornaments of metaphora and metonymy), willfully applied in accord with well-known rhetorical conventions by a well-educated and well-stocked mind. This is how such compositions work. We need our inventory well-stored, our memory fully attentive, and we work and work away at the text in the way that a jeweller (or other master craftsman) works gold. We "worry" the text (another meaning of sollicitudo), inventing our own meditation from a meeting of its materials and those of our own mnemonic inventories. "Invention" in a rhetorical culture is not primarily caused by a spontaneous overflow of powerful feelings, nor is it a rapture of the unconscious mind. It comes via homophonies and visual patterns, oppositions and correspondences of figure and form that arouse the mind to look and listen—and only then to construct its meanings upon the locations they provide.

Notes

1. See Mary Carruthers, *The Book of Memory*, rev. ed. (Cambridge: Cambridge University Press, 1992).

2. The only edition of this work is in Jean Leclercq's admirable study, *La Spiritualité de Pierre de Celle* (Paris: Vrin, 1946), 231–39. References to this work are cited by page and line numbers from this edition. All translations are mine.

3. *OED*, s.v. *punctuation*, 1.

4. Varro, *De lingua latina*, 6.46, ed. and trans. R. G. Kent (Cambridge, MA: Harvard University Press, 1938). See also *The Book of Memory*, 48–49.

5. See in particular Eugene Vance, "Roland and the Poetics of Memory," in *Textual Strategies: Perspectives in Post-Structural Criticism*, ed. Josue V. Harari (Ithaca: Cornell University Press, 1979), 374–403; Louise Fradenburg, "'Voice Memorial': Loss and Reparation in Chaucer's Poetry," *Exemplaria* 2 (1990): 169–202; Jody Enders, *Rhetoric and the Origins of Medieval Drama* (Ithaca: Cornell University Press, 1992). I discuss the violent, sexual images recommended in Thomas Bradwardine's art of memory in *The Book of Memory*, 130–37.

6. See esp. Henri-Irénée Marrou, *Histoire de l'education dans l'antiquité* (Paris: Seuil, 1948), 240–42; Augustine describes, in the first book of *Confessions*, the whippings that accompanied his memorizing of texts. The standard iconography of Grammar included a switch in her hand for beating her students. Barbara Hanawalt, *Growing up in Medieval London* (New York: Oxford University Press, 1993), quotes a typical student's lament from 1500 about the sharpness of birch twigs (pp. 84–85)—social attitudes towards the necessity of corporal "impression" of elementary learning evidently had not changed from ancient times.

7. I discuss the mnemotechnical aspects of this poem, and its layout in Cambridge, University Library Ii.3.26, in "'Ut pictura poesis': The Rhetoric of Verbal and Visual Images," *Mentalities/Mentalités* 7:1 (Fall, 1990): 1–6.

8. Robert A. Kaster, *Guardians of Language: The Grammarian and Society in Late Antiquity* (Berkeley: University of California Press, 1988), 16–17; the citation is to Galen, Περιεθῶν, 4.

9. "Triplici studio tirones Christi probantur sub uexillo militantes in cella, afflicitione scilicet corporali qua carnis lasciuia infrenatur, lectione Novi et Veteris Testamenti qua anima pascitur, oratione compunctiua pro peccatis qua spiritus ad Deum subleuatur" (231.1–4).

10. Prologue, *St. Benedict's Rule for Monasteries*, trans. Leonard J. Doyle (Collegeville, MN: Liturgical Press, 1948).

11. The most eloquent English proponent of this emphasis within monasticism is R. A. Markus: see his two studies, *Saeculum: History and Society in the Theology of St. Augustine*, rev. ed. (Cambridge: Cambridge University Press, 1988) and *The End of Ancient Christianity* (Cambridge: Cambridge University Press, 1990).

12. "Exarmat enim propugnacula sua *mille clypeis pendentibus ex eis* [cf. Sg. 4:4] qui non uacat lectionibus diuinis. O quam cito et sine labor capietur ciuitatula cellae, nisi se defenderit auxilio Dei et scuto diuinae paginae! . . . Sume nihilominus de armario librorum missilia quibus percussus percussorem tuum repercutias" (233.25–36).

13. A number of examples of these common tropes for the memory store are collected in *The Book of Memory*, chapter 1. It was an ideal of monasticism that one's memory be a library of texts: for example, Didymus, the blind Greek expositor of Scripture, whom Cassiodorus admired because he had so stored away all the authors and texts of Scripture in the library of his memory ("in memoriae suae bibliotheca") that he could immediately tell you in which part of the codex any bit of text could be found; see Cassiodorus, *Institutiones*, 1.5.2.

14. H. G. Liddell and R. Scott, *A Greek-English Lexicon*, s.v. melet-.

15. I discuss the derivation of the English idiom "by rote" in *The Book of Memory*, 252.

16. Though I quarrel with a number of its conclusions and emphases, and though she omitted a great deal of pertinent medieval material, Yates's book remains important for the study of late medieval mnemonic technique: Frances A. Yates, *The Art of Memory* (London: Routledge, 1966). An essential recent study, which corrects many of Yates's characterizations of Renaissance (especially Italian) memory arts is Lina Bolzoni, *La stanza della memoria: Modelli letterari e iconografici nell'éta della stampa* (Torino: Einaudi, 1995).

17. These ideas were expounded by Augustine: see Janet Coleman, *Ancient and Medieval Memories* (Cambridge: Cambridge University Press, 1992). Two earlier essays that contain much good judgment are R. A. Markus, "Augustine on Signs," *Phronesis* 2 (1957): 60–83, and G. B. Matthews, "Augustine on Speaking from Memory," in *Augustine: A Collection of Essays*, ed. R. A. Markus (New York: Anchor Doubleday, 1972), 168–75. The concept of "image" also has a resonance in rhetorical training: Augustine's conception of these terms has as much to do with the rhetorical usage as with the various philosophical traditions with which he was familiar.

18. Sandra Blakeslee, reporting on the research chiefly of Joseph LeDoux of New York University and Hanna and Antonio Damasio of the University of Iowa; *New York Times*, 6 Dec. 1994, sec. B, 5, 11. See also Antonio Damasio, *Descartes' Error: Emotion, Reason, and the Human Brain* (New York: G. P. Putnam, 1994).

19. "Qua carnis lascivia infrenatur" (231.2); "spiritus fornicationis" (231.23).

20. Conference 10.13–14: "Cum enim capitulum cuiuslibet psalmi mens nostra conceperit, insensibiliter eo subtracto ad alterius scripturae textum nesciens stupensque deuoluitur. Cumque illud in semet ipsua coeperit uolutare, necdum illo ad integrum uentilato oborta alterius testimonii memoria meditationem materiae prioris excludit. De hac quoque ad alteram subintrante alia meditatione transfertur, et ita animus semper de psalmo rotatus ad psalmum, de euangelii textu ad apostoli transiliens lectionem, de hac quoque ad prophetica deuolutus eloquia et exinde ad quasdam spiritales delatus historias per omne scripturarum corpus instabilis uagusque iactatur, nihil pro arbitrio suo praeualens uel abicere uel tenere nec pleno quicquam iudicio et examinatione finire, palpator tantummodo spiritalium sensuum ac degustator, non generator nec possessor effectus. . . . Cum orat, psalmum aut aliquam recolit lectionem. Cum decantat, aliud quid meditatur quam textus ipsius continet psalmi. . . . Tria sunt quae uagam mentem stabilem faciunt, vigilae, meditatio et oratio, quarum adsiduitas et iugio intentio conferunt animae stabilem firmitatem." See Jean Cassien, *Conférences*, ed. E. Pichery, 3 vols., Sources chrétiennes (Paris: Éditions Cerf, 1955–59), 2:94–95. Subsequent references are to this text. The translation is my own, though I consult the French trans-

lation of Pichery and the English of Colm Luibheid (John Cassian, *Conferences*, trans. Colm Luibheid [New York: Paulist Press, 1985]).

21. The importance of the notion of being "stabilis" in Cassian's thought and its relationship to concepts in rhetoric is the subject of a good analysis by Conrad Leyser, "*Lectio divina, oratio pura*: Rhetoric and the Techniques of Asceticism in the 'Conferences' of John Cassian," in *Modelli di santità e modelli di comportamento: contrasti, intersezioni, complementarità*, ed. M. Caffiero, F. S. Barcellona, and G. Barone (Turin: Rosenberg and Sellier, 1994), 79–105.

22. "Cellula quae meminit est cellula deliciarum," Geoffrey of Vinsauf, *Poetria nova*, line 1972; ed. E. Faral, *Les arts poétiques du XIIe et du XIIIe siècle* (1924; repr. Paris: Champion, 1953).

23. The best known instances include Augustine's regret at how the scene of Dido's death made him weep (*Confessions* 1.13–14), and Jerome's vision of being expelled from Heaven because he was a Ciceronian rather than a Christian (*Epistolae* 22).

24. Conference 14.13: "De hac ipsa re, unde tibi purgationis maxima nascitur desperatio, citum satis atque efficax remedium poterit oboriri, si eandem diligentiam atque instantiam, quam te in illis saecularibus studiis habuisse dixisti, ad spiritalium scripturarum uoleris lectionem meditationemque transferre." (conference 14.12).

25. The study of H.-I. Marrou, *Histoire de l'education dans l'antiquité* is essential. For an English translation see *A History of Education in Antiquity*, trans. George Lamb (1956; repr. Madison: University of Wisconsin Press, 1982). See also his *St. Augustin et le fin de la culture antique* (Paris: Boccard, 1938). A good study in English is Stanley Bonner, *Education in Ancient Rome* (Berkeley: University of California Press, 1977).

26. Conference 14.13: "Quae cum profunde alteque conceperit atque in illis fuerit enutrita, uel expelli priores sensim poterunt uel penitus aboleri. Vacare enim cunctis cogitationibus humana mens non potest, et ideo quamdiu spiritalibus studiis non fuerit occupata, necesse est eam illis quae pridem didicit inplicari. Quamdiu enim non habuerit quo recurrat et indefessos exerceat motus, necesse est ut ad illa quibus ad infantia inbuta est conlabatur eaque semper reuoluat quae longo usu ac meditatione concepit. Vt ergo haec in te scientia spiritalis perpetua soliditate roboretur . . . ut sensibus tuis inuiscerata quodammodo et perspecta atque palpata condatur. . . . Si itaque haec diligenter excepta

et in recessu mentis condita atque indicta fuerint taciturnitate signata, postea ut uina quaedam suaue olentia et laetificantia cor hominis . . . cum magna sui fragrantia de uase tui pectoris proferentur . . . Atque ita fiet ut non solum omnis directio ac meditatio cordis tui, uerum etiam cunctae euagationes atque discursus cogitationum tuarum sint tibi diuinae legis sancta et incessabilis ruminatio" (2:199–201).

27. I analyze the crucial role of "murmur" and "silent" reading (*legere tacite*) in mnemonic technique in *The Book of Memory*, 169–74.

28. Conference 14.13: "de experientiae uenis . . . redundabunt fluentaque continua uelut de quadam abysso tui cordis effundent" (2:201).

29. Conference 1.18: "Quod exercitium cordis non incongrue molarum similitudini conparatur, quas meatus aquarum praeceps impetu rotante prouoluit. Quae nullatenus quidem cessare possunt ab opere suo aquarum inpulsibus circumactae: in eius uero qui praeest situm est potestate, utrumnam triticum malit an hordeum loliumue comminui. Illud quippe est procul dubio conmolendum, quod ingestum ab illo fuerit cui operis illius cura commissa est. . . . Si enim ut diximus ad sanctarum scripturarum meditationem iugiter recurramus ac memoriam nostram ad recordationem spiritalium rerum . . . necesse est ut ortae cogitationes exinde spiritales. . . . Sin uero desidia seu neglegentia superati uitiis et otiosis confabulationibus occupemur . . . consequenter exinde uelut quaedam zizaniorum species generata operationem quoque nostro cordi noxiam ministrabit" (1:99).

30. A. R. Luria, *The Mind of a Mnemonist*, trans. Lynn Solotaroff (New York: Basic Books, 1968), 66–73.

31. Notice that, basically, the trope rings changes upon the syllable *mel-* preceeding the various vowels, *a, i, e, o*. This is an extremely common means both of learning and "alphabetizing" (that is "inventorying") through the Middle Ages: see *The Book of Memory*, 120–21. In that same book, I describe families of tropes for trained memory, including honey and bees, the role of melancholy, and the basic mnemonic technique of "dividing" a long work into memory-sized bits, like the limbs of a body or verses of a poem.

32. On mental fornication, especially the "straying of thoughts" and "speculations" of "words and names," see esp. Conference 14.11. It is probably worth mentioning that the concept in Cassian's time meant what we would now call indiscriminately "sleeping around" with pros-

titutes. In his discussion of *curiositas* as a vice of the mind, Augustine calls it "concupiscentia oculis," meaning the "eye" of the mind: see *Confessions* 10.35. Augustine's concept is very close to that of Cassian, but I have chosen to focus on Cassian in part because Augustine's discussion is better known now, and in part because Cassian is so clear about the cognitive processes involved in *curiositas*.

33. This was the sermon which convinced Geoffrey of Auxerre, already a cleric, to enter monastic life. See the introductory remarks of Jean Leclercq to his edition of this sermon, "Ad clericos de conversione": *Sancti Bernardi Opera*, ed. J. Leclercq, C. H. Talbot, and H. Rochais, 8 vols. (Rome: Editiones Cistercienses, 1957–77), 4:61. Further references to this work, cited hereafter as "Ad clericos," are to this edition.

34. "Quidni doleam ventrem memoriae, ubi tanta congesta est putredo?" (*Ad clericos*, 3.4 [4:75]). The translation is my own.

35. Coleman, *Ancient and Medieval Memories*, 175, 186. While in the main Coleman addresses monastic attitudes towards memory with sympathetic judiciousness, her account, it seems to me, suffers from her disengagement with the praxis of prayer—memory in action, not just in theory.

36. *Ad clericos* 16.29.

37. *Ad clericos* 15.28.

38. "Quomodo enim a memoria mea excidet vita mea? Membrana vilis et tenuis atramentum forte ebibit; qua deinceps arte delebitur? Non enim superficie tenus tinxit; sed prorsus totam intinxit. Frustra conarer eradere: ante scinditur charta quam caracteres miseri deleantur. Ipsam enim forte memoriam delere posset oblivio, ut videlicet, mente captus, eorum non meminerim, quae commisi. Ceterum, ut memoria integra maneat et ipsius maculae diluantur, quae novacula possit efficere? Solus utique sermo vivus et efficax, et penetrabilior omni gladio ancipiti: 'dimittuntur tibi peccata tua.' . . . Huius indulgentia delet peccatum, non quidem ut a memoria excidat, sed ut quod prius inesse pariter et inficere consuevisset, sic de cetero insit memoriae, ut eam nullatenus decoloret. . . . Tolle damnationem, tolle timorem, tolle confusionem, quae quidem omnia plena remissio tollit, et non modo non oberunt, sed et cooperantur in bonum" (*Ad clericos* 15.28 [4:102–4]).

39. Even sexual and scatalogical material can be used, so long as one does not get "confused" by it: the fifteenth-century master, Peter

of Ravenna (also known as Petrus Tommai), said that he marked his memory places with images of seductive women, for "these greatly stimulate my memory"—but this method was not suitable, he cautions, for those who hate women (i. e. have the wrong "stance") or those without control (who are subject to the vice of curiosity): see his *Foenix domini Petri Ravenatis memoriae magistri* (Venice, 1491). Peter's practice may be seen as a turn on an old and well-known ascetic exercise in withstanding temptation—in this case, an exercise against "mental fornication."

40. Peter of Celle, *De conscientia*, prologue, lines 3–5: "religiosa mens religiosa curiositate quaerit de religione conscientiae." The only complete edition of this work is in Leclercq, *La spiritualité de Pierre de Celle*, 193–230.

41. Anselm, "Meditation 2: a lament for virginity unhappily lost," *The Prayers and Meditations of St. Anselm*, trans. Benedicta Ward (London: Penguin, 1973), 227–29.

42. Job 10:21–22: "Antequam vadam, et non revertar, ad terram tenebrosam, et opertam mortis caligine: Terram miseriae et tenebrarum, ubi umbra mortis et nullus ordo, sed sempiternus horror inhabitat."

43. "Sede in cella quasi in paradiso; proice post tergum de memoria totum mundum, cautus ad cogitationes, quasi bonus piscator ad pisces. Una via est in psalmis; hanc ne dimittas. Si non potes omnia, qui venisti fervore novicio, nunc in hoc, nunc illo loco psallere in spiritu et intelligere mente stude, et cum ceperis vagari legendo, ne desistas, sed festina intelligendo emendare; pone te ante omnia in presentia Dei cum timore et tremore, quasi qui stat in conspectu imperatoris; destrue te totum et sede quasi pullus, contentus ad gratiam Dei, quia, nisi mater donet, nec sapit nec habet quod comedat." St. Romuald's advice is quoted in Bruno of Querfort, *Vita quinque fratrum*, ed. Reinhard Kade, Monumenta Germaniae Historica, Scriptores 15, part 2, pp. 709–38 at 738.23–30.

44. St. Romuald was the subject of a biography by the great contemplative monk, St. Peter Damian, a generation after his death, and what we know of Romuald comes mainly from this source, for he left no writings of his own. The account of his meditational method quoted here is by one of his disciples, Bruno of Querfort, who went as a missionary to Russia, where he was martyred in 1009.

45. Translated in Appendix A of *The Book of Memory*, 261–66.

46. Quintilian likens finding the "places" of argument to finding the places where fish, or game, lie hidden: *Institutio oratoria*, 5.10.20–22. A similar metaphor is found in Greek; see *The Book of Memory*, 62, 247, and figure 28.

CHAPTER TWO

The Book as Flesh and Fetish in Richard de Bury's *Philobiblon*

Michael Camille

That our intent and purpose, therefore, may be known to posterity as well as to our contemporaries; and that we may for ever stop the perverse tongues of gossipers as far as we are concerned, we have published a little treatise . . . [that] will purge from the accusation of excess the love we have held towards books and will proclaim the purpose of our eager devotion and make clearer than light the circumstances of our undertaking. And since it treats chiefly the love of books, we have chosen after the fashion of the ancient Romans, fondly to name it by a Greek word, *Philobiblon*.[1]

On 24 January 1345 on his fifty-eighth birthday and only three months before his death, Richard de Bury, bishop of Durham, completed the treatise that has established his posthumous reputation as medieval Europe's greatest book collector. In its numerous reprintings since the fifteenth century the *Philobiblon* has become a favorite of those "who are fully susceptible to the delights and exquisite sensibilities of that sweet madness called bibliomania."[2] According to Dibdin's eighteenth-century satire *Bibliomania or Book Madness*, Richard de Bury was the very first "eminent character who appears to have been infected with this disease," and later students of the malady, like F. Somner Merry-weather, describe his "unbosoming . . . all the inward rapture of love" and using language "that is not always chaste."[3] The bibliophilia described by these antiquarians as an eccentric passion we are more likely today to see as a perversion. For the contemporary philosopher Gilles Deleuze, the pervert is "someone who introduces desire into an entirely different system and makes it play, within this system, the role of an internal limit."[4] The limits of the bibliophile's desire are problematic precisely because his objects are everywhere, circulating in the culture as powerful public symbols of knowledge and power. Like the pedophile and the necrophile, the bibliophile is forced to negotiate surreptitiously a desire for bodies that, though ubiquitous and highly visible, are nonetheless marked off by social convention as "out of bounds"—pre-sexually pure in the case of the child or post-sexually dead in that of the corpse. Both these phantasmic bodies, child and corpse, pre-pubescent and post-mortem, are, as we shall see, enfolded and encrypted among many others, including the bishop's own, within the pages of his philological fantasy.

Scholars of the Middle Ages have tended to see the book as a closed object, as a *summa*, or what Derrida called "the idea of a totality." But once opened the book's metaphors become those of exteriority and interiority, surface and depth, of covering and exposure, of taking apart and putting together. For Susan Stewart, the phrase "between covers" calls to mind "the titillation of intellectual and sexual reproduction."[5] The *Philobiblon* tells us far more about this nub of interrelated desires for books (as bodies as well as progenitors) than previous interpreters have noted. One exception is Carolyn Dinshaw, who, in *Chaucer's Sexual Poetics*, describes how much de Bury's investment in books protects against "violations of property, territory, lineage and family—against violations of the patriarchy."[6] As an art historian interested in how the illuminated book, but also manuscript culture more generally, perpetuates itself between covers, I want in this essay to explore how this treatise might engage with actual practices of writing, decorating, binding, and ultimately also reading fourteenth-century manuscripts. De Bury becomes a test-case, although an exceptional one, for the interpenetration of corporeality and codicology that is crucial to understanding the late medieval book. The final colophon of the *Philobiblon* states that it was finished on the bishop's birthday, "the fifty-eighth year of our age exactly completed" (181). This coincidence between the primal appearance of his own body and the completion of his book is part of a simultaneous incorporation and projection that might, initially at least, be addressed using the concept of fetishism.

Fetishizing the Book

Case 99. X., aged twenty, inverted sexually. Only loved men with a large bushy mustache. One day he met a man who answered his ideal. He invited him into his home, but was unspeakably disappointed when this man removed an artificial mustache. Only when the visitor put the ornament on the upper lip again, did he exercise his charm over X. once more and restore him to the full possession of his virility.[7]

The fetish shall be discussed here, not in the anthropological sense of a totem, nor in the Marxist sense of the capitalist commodity, but rather in the Freudian sense of the eroticized substitute object, like the mustache sought by Dr. Krafft-Ebing's invert, which need not be a real thing but be more a provocation to desire and possession. Constructed by the intensity of the scopophilic male gaze under the threat of castration, the fetish in current psychoanalytic theory "stands for some aspect of the separated mother."[8] As a dehumanized replacement for the lost object of the mother's penis, this split-off, idealized substitute becomes the source for sexual excitement. The specific means—shoes, corsets, leather, rubber, facial hair—whereby the fetishist, traumatized by the lost phallus, turns to another less threatening object that can represent it, might seem at first to call to mind the manufactured things and textures of modernity rather than anything medieval. Yet no object was more painstakingly manufactured in the Middle Ages than the manuscript. The medieval imaginary also certainly constructed illicit desires in terms of what modern experts on fetishism describe as a "hypersensitivity to the sexuality of things" or objects. Sins such as *concupiscentia*, *luxuria*, and *avaritia* were represented in public imagery from the early thirteenth century onwards as persons perversely interacting with things. *Avarice*, for example, is a man placing possessions (usually money and clothes) in a chest. As carved on the cathedral fronts of Notre Dame in Paris and Amiens cathedral (fig. 1), these images of sins have to be seen not only as traditional depictions of the vices to be avoided but also as part of the construction of a new self-confessing identity, mediated through those very illicit objects of desire they were meant to refuse.[9] Although it might seem at first quite anachronistic to apply the concept of fetishism to such distant historical practices as book-collecting in the Middle Ages, I have found it useful as a way of exploring the psychic fixations and displacements that are evident throughout de Bury's text. As William Pietz has argued, the fetish is always "a historical object" which is also "personalized in the sense that beyond its status as a collective social object it evokes an intensely personal response from individuals."[10] This split between what the fetishist really wants to do with the object and the actual social status of that object is one of the crucial dynamics of the fetish. In the Middle Ages, as I shall argue, it was seen as quite normal to have an intensely personal response to books. As Pietz explains, there was no problem in medieval culture with material objects bearing exceptional magical power, such as the sacraments of the church. One has to distinguish this universally accepted semi-magical erotics of the object from de Bury's strange, surrogate relationship to his uncannily animated volumes, a relationship he is at pains to disavow throughout the *Philobiblon*.

Richard d'Aungerville was born into a knightly family near Bury St. Edmunds in 1287, orphaned at an early age and brought up by his uncle, who was a rector at a grammar school. At Oxford, where he studied arts and theology (without incepting) from 1302 to 1312, his academic career was undistinguished, and according to Adam of Murimuth he was always "mediocriter literatus."[11] He soon gave up the schools for the court, however, gaining in 1322 the position of tutor to the young Edward of Windsor, the future Edward III.[12] A straightforward, biographically-driven psycho-history might argue that the objects of scholarship—books—became the lost relics and thus the fervid fetishes of de Bury's own unfulfilled scholastic ambitions. But I do not want to attempt this type of analysis, which would (simplistically, I think) seek to link de Bury's early childhood loss of his mother with his later fetishistic reparation of that maternal body. Rather than de Bury himself, I am interested in his text and what it can tell us about how books as objects could become sites of subjectivity, self-embodiment, and even perversion in fourteenth-century culture.

Certain aspects of de Bury's life, like his enormous wealth and political power, are, however, crucial in understanding his bibliophilia. When he attacks those who "carelessly spend a few years of hot youth, alternating with the excesses of vice, and when the passions are calmed, and they have attained the capacity of discerning truth so difficult to discover, they soon become involved in worldly affairs and retire, bidding farewell to the schools of philosophy" (101), he is not only separating the realms of the body and the book that will later become hopelessly mixed-up in this treatise, he is also describing his own early career. When his princely pupil became king in January 1327, de Bury was given important administrative positions as Cofferer, then Treasurer of the Wardrobe, and, shortly afterwards, Clerk of the Privy Seal. Around 1330 his illustrious diplomatic career began. His many travels, as ambassador to the papal court at Avignon in 1333 (where he met Petrarch) and many times to Paris (his favorite book-buying paradise), gave him every opportunity to acquire volumes to add to his growing collection. While at Avignon in 1333 he heard that he had been appointed Bishop of Durham, but this appointment to the wealthiest see in the land did not prevent him from continuing his political career as Lord Treasurer and then Lord Chancellor. Although his court was a meeting place for the foremost Oxford scholars, lovers of "English subtleties" and "calculations," de Bury himself left no major works apart from the *Philobiblon*, and even his authorship of this treatise has been disputed. His distaste for administration, what Beryl Smalley calls his "magnificent carelessness," meant that he left his estate in such bad financial shape that his vast collection of books, rather than going to endow an Oxford college as he outlines in the closing chapters of the *Philobiblon*, was instead sold off by his executors to pay his debts.[13]

The material traces of de Bury's obsession have mostly disappeared. None of the numerous manuscripts of the *Philobiblon* itself can be associated with de Bury, most being copies of the fifteenth century. No catalogue of his library has survived, and only three of what must have been hundreds of his beloved volumes have subsequently been traced.[14] Only two other material monuments of his patronage are still in existence; the first is the second of his great episcopal seals of 1335, showing him vested beneath an elaborate architectural canopy. This was one of the most artistically advanced and visually splendid seals yet produced in England. It is an index of the bishop's role as guardian of his flock, his political power and his spiritual prestige, though books, not being episcopal symbols, are nowhere present (fig. 2).[15] More pertinent is an oak chest, now in the

Burrell Collection, Glasgow, painted on the inside lid with snap-ping dragons and a scaly, sword-wielding babewyn. Revealing its signs of identity (the family coats of arms) only when opened, and with the kind of magical protective and humorous imagery that one finds in the margins of contemporary manuscripts, it is like a book itself (fig. 3).[16] This may be one of the very chests which housed the contents of his library, or the one that was opened at his death by his eager executors, expecting to find treasure to pay his debts, but found to contain only linen and hair-breeches.[17]

How then can we imagine de Bury's library? The fourteenth-century library was not the visibly stratified space of order, the disembodied, panoptic display that we know today but was much more intimate, interactive, and corporeal. The whole his-tory, development, and, to some extent, the institutional aims of the modern library have been to exclude the body from the site of reading, to make a silent and desomatized optics of the biblioteca the simulacrum of purely mental experience, a process that will only accelerate in the future with the increasing in-corporeality of the electronic word. By contrast the medieval li-brary was a site of performance, where people left their traces in their books without fear of censure. They marked them, doodled in them, defaced them, chewed them, tore them up, and even slept with them, as in fourteenth-century images showing books being used in bed, one of the few private spaces in medieval culture (fig. 4). These are the very practices of which de Bury vehemently disapproves and which he describes in lurid de-tail later in his treatise. Contemporaries would have found the Bishop's tastes strange, not so much in his interaction with his volumes, but in his distance from them and in his desire to keep them closed.

The book has lost much of its corporeal, communicative, and erotic associations with the speaking/sucking mouth, the gestur-ing/probing hand, or the opening/closing body. Reading for the medieval literate was charged with these associations that made every turn of the page an act of intense interpenetration and one resonant with sensations, from the feel of the flesh and hair side of the parchment on one's fingertips to the lubricious labial mouthing of the words with one's throat and tongue. The way medieval books were bound with thongs between stamped leather or wooden boards, held shut with metal studs, encased in hide belts, and snapped shut with buckle-like clasps made them mysterious. Also suggestive was the way they were displayed with their backsides uppermost on desks when taken out of their locked chests and turned for delectation, quite literally on the moving "reading wheel" (fig. 5), like the turning wheels that broke not the spines of volumes but the backs and bones of transgressors of law in the public squares of cities. All this made them into clunky and physically intimidating objects. This aspect is again something elided in de Bury's text, which emphasizes not so much their physical presence but their absent voices. They are, in the very opening chapter, *thesaurus desiderabilis sapientiae* ("the desirable treasure of wisdom") already shut up in the chest.

For most literates in the culture however, the very act of reading was a libidinal experience, of penetrating the bound volume, that dangerously ductile opening and shutting thing, with numerous puns and jokes on the "two-leaved book" already in circulation.[18] The result was a promiscuous interpenetration of books, not only with the bodies that read them, but also with those that were excluded from them. Perhaps only today, with the fast-approaching "death of the book," are we able to begin to appreciate and partially recover the cultural history of this long-submerged desire. For when I open a medieval manuscript, and this is different from opening a printed book, I am conscious not only of the manu-script, the bodily handling of materials in production, writing, illumination, but also how in its subsequent reception, the parchment has been penetrated; how it has acquired grease-stains, thumb-marks, erasures, drops of sweat;

suffered places where images have been kissed away by devout lips or holes from various eating animals. In short, humans, animals, and insects have left the imprints of countless bodies upon it. Every book is a relic of countless bodily ejaculations. This is also attested in the way people handled books. At this period, at least in the large chained libraries of collegiate institutions, one entered most books from behind. According to Malcolm Parkes, the opening of books from the back can be inferred from the direction of clasps on medieval bindings and the position of colophons and labels on the back covers. "At St. Augustine's Abbey, Canterbury, novices were instructed to take a book in the left hand (covered by the sleeve of the habit) and turn the pages with the right, a practice which would encourage the habit of opening the book from the back."[19]

By contrast, de Bury's body seems at first a long way from the pages he describes. None of the numerous manuscripts of his treatise can be attributed to his own day, let alone his own hand (he surely would have dictated it to one of his many copyists anyway). In "writing" his treatise he was committing to parchment nothing like a personal confession of an obsession, but a highly formalized and rhetorically ornate tract in a style he calls "levissimo stylo modernorum." He also deployed a very formal letter-writing mode known as the *cursus curiae romanae*. This utilized a strict system of rhythmical clausulae, in which not only each clause but each sentence ended in a defined way.[20] No English translation can give a sense of the magisterial music of the Latin, its syncopated symmetry and its meandering, varying velocity. The purpose of these elaborate procedures of stresses falling on the ends of sentences was to embellish the authority of the spoken word at a time when most reading was done aloud. In this sense the *Philobiblon* was a book made manifest through de Bury's own body, as its Latin phrases are declaimed in a highly personal and hortatory self-consciousness that plays on the artifice of spoken utterance. Those sentences expressing his indignation at, for example, the eating habits of the greedy clergy ("Greges et vellera, fruges et horrea, porri et olera, potus et patera") are like tongue-twisters, designed to make the mouth salivate with all their movement. This is another disjunction evident throughout the *Philobiblon*, between the fantasies of seeing and hearing, between the optical obsession to view writing as dead (a kind of silence) and the urge to eat, devour, and ingest it as living speech. At mealtimes de Bury had his favorite works read aloud to him as he ate, as if to synchronize the ingestion of intellectual and bodily fruits and sublimate the need for physical contact with the flesh through rhythmic pulsations on the ear. Describing his search for volumes all over Europe in chapter 8 and immediately after the famous passage about the superiority of "English subtlety" to Parisian "antiquity," he relates how this truth was "instantly poured still fresh into our ears, ungarbled by any babbler, unmutilated by any trifler, but passing straight from the purest of wine presses into the vats of our memory to be clarified."[21] De Bury had emphasized the sensorial lubricity of this delightful distillation in the very first chapter:

> For the meaning of the voice ["virtus vocis"] perishes with the sound; truth latent in the mind is wisdom that is hid and treasure that is not seen; but truth which shines forth in books desires to manifest itself to every impressionable sense ["omni discipliniabli sensui"]. It commends itself to the sight when it is read, to the hearing when it is heard, and moreover, in a manner, to the touch, when it suffers itself to be transcribed, bound, corrected and preserved. (19)

Notably, touch is only briefly described here, and only in the construction of the volume, not as part of its handling or reception by de Bury as its possessor. This avoidance of interaction with books throughout the treatise we might see as a psychic "blind-spot," a scotomization of any unwelcome perception of the object of desire. Also part of this denial of the object is the fact that in the whole of the *Philobiblon* there is not one description of an individual volume or a particular book acquired by the bishop at much cost or effort. The author refers often to great authors of the past, ancient and modern, but as though they were speaking to him in his library rather than being bound between boards on parchment pages that he has actually to open to read. There are no actual books in this treatise on the love of books, only the echo of voices.

Michel Foucault puts the relation between desire and the library most succinctly: "The imaginary is not formed in opposition to reality as its denial or compensation; it grows among signs, from book to book, in the interstice of repetitions and commentaries; it is born and takes place in the interval between books. It is a phenomenon of the library."[22] As well as being part of the ruse of avoiding the accusation of bibliophilia, stressing that the bishop is a lover of learning rather than of specific physical objects, de Bury appropriates these desired objects as already incorporated into the body. Most citations are of the type: "As Aristotle, the sun of science, has said of logic in his book *De pomo*. . . ." This is typical of a system of references that cites in order to embody the ancient author's wisdom as part of his own discourse. This again displaces the fetishist from the objects of his desire, which are lost once they are cited. Nor is there any account or description of the place and storage of the vast numbers of volumes we know de Bury possessed. It is from other sources, such as a recorded text on a plaque once in Durham cathedral, that we learn how no less than five carts were needed to transport his library, how his dormitory was so strewn with volumes in every corner that it was impossible for any person to enter without placing his feet upon some book.[23] The excess of this can be judged by the fact that at the papal court in Avignon during de Bury's time, the number of books owned by the lesser clergy was nine each. Merton College Library boasted fewer than two hundred volumes at this date, and most private collections suggest a similar number.[24] The history of art-collecting, which has become so important in recent art history, tends to focus on the period post-1500 and for some reason excludes books, as though these could not be objects of desire, only of knowledge.

The problem for de Bury was squaring what he called his "hot" and "ecstatic love" of books with the traditional Christian renunciation of the vanity of material objects and the "wants of the perishing body." It entailed a massive evasion of the book's materiality and the construction of the treatise around a highly artificial rhetoric that only surreptitiously reveals anything like a corporeal attitude to the book. The ostensibly pedagogical function of his treatise means he tends to focus on books as finished, not as made. But we should not forget that books were the focus of intense labor, expensive materials, luxury decoration, and often lavish stamped leather or silk bindings. The book was an object of great value in the fourteenth century; it could cost as much as the finest horse. This was the period when the burgeoning book trade produced professionally the expensive items that de Bury travelled throughout Europe to acquire. They were no longer the spiritual tools of communal meditation that they had been in the monastery, where, as the bishop himself nostalgically laments in chapter 5 "some used to write them with their own hands between the hours of prayer, and gave to the making of books such intervals as they could secure and the times appointed for the recreation of the body" (53). This direct relation between the making of bodies and the making of books was different in the fourteenth century when most new volumes, purchased from *libraires* in Paris or from stationers in London, were commodities now collected by individuals as well as communities. Churchmen like Richard de Fournival, chancellor of Amiens cathedral, had in fact created one of the earliest private libraries in the middle of the previous century.[25] But whereas Fournival's *Biblionomia* outlines how he arranged his books in three rooms as a "garden" of knowledge, open, he claims, to the public, de Bury's treatise is an inward-turning and more occluded expression of personal possession in which the fetish object is hidden rather than revealed by language.

Engendering the Book

Desire, or love as the medievals understood it and Andreas Capellanus described it in his *De amore*, begins with vision, the gateway to the mind. "Love is a certain inborn suffering ["passio innata"] which results from the sight of ["visione"] and uncontrolled thinking about ["immoderata cogitatione"] the beauty of the other sex."[26] De Bury's position as one of the leading prelates of the realm gave him full opportunity to engage not only in the gynophobic misogyny of his contemporaries, but also in a gynophilia which is just as scopic as any love-treatise of the period. He is indeed somewhat obsessed with vision. His detractors are denigrated in terms of eye metaphors ("blind men judging of colors"; "let not bats venture to speak of light"; let them "cease to discuss hidden things that are not revealed to the eyes of men"). Chapter 1 of de Bury's treatise, as well as including the famous passage "in books I find the dead as if they were alive," goes on to describe the perception of books as being more permanent in the visual than in the aural realm. "But the written truth of books, not transient but permanent, plainly offers itself to be observed, and by means of the pervious spherules of the eyes, passing through the vestibule of perception [in the Latin this is the more scientific term "vestibula sensus communis"] and the courts of imagination ["imaginationis atria"] enters the chamber of intellect, taking its place in the couch of memory ["cubili memoriae"], where it engenders the eternal truth of the mind ["congenerit veritatem"]."[27] This architectural, domestic metaphor of the "house of memory," the moving from exterior to interior, is reminiscent of the way that perception was seen in terms of the "doors of seeing and hearing" according to Richard de Fournival, and also diagrammed in more scholarly Latin treatises on optics in the fourteenth century.

It also culminates with the notion of engendering that parallels the sperm's gestation in the womb as medievals understood it (needing no fertilizing egg). The optical experience of the lover's gaze which gives birth to thoughts is made possible through the interpenetration of body and book. De Bury's sin is a sin of looking. In psychoanalytic terms reading and writing are, in the words of André Green, "sublimations, which means that the underlying partial drives are inhibited from attaining their goals and as a result have to be displaced and desexualized. Once broken down into their constituent parts, those partial drives have to do with scopophilia. . . . The book cover, the binding function as garments . . . reading has a great deal to do with voyeurism."[28] Just as fetishism is a product of the anxiety of not looking or daring to look at the mother's body, recovering that suppressed object entails de Bury's holding on to that metaphorical maternity by refusing to behold the book's body, either to see or touch its protective coverings or decorative embellishments.

In his Prologue de Bury also attacks in gynecological terms those youths who leave the study of the liberal arts for the more lucrative mechanical ones: "Thus Mother Church conceiving sons is compelled to miscarry, nay some misshapen monster is born untimely from her womb." In chapter 4 the books make their own complaint against the clergy already promoted calling them "a generation of vipers destroying their own parents." They are as ungrateful offspring:

> In sooth, while still untrained and helpless ye crept up to us, ye spake as children, ye thought as children, ye cried as children and begged to be partakers of our milk. But we being straightaway moved by your tears gave you the breast of grammar to suck, which

ye plied continually with teeth and tongue, until ye lost your native barbarousness and learned to speak with our tongues the mighty things of God. And next we clad you with the goodly garments of philosophy, rhetoric and dialectic, of which we had and have a store, while ye were naked as a tablet to be painted on ["tabula depingenda"]. (35)

These are, of course, traditional tropes which had long linked grammar and sexual generation. Grammar is shown breast feeding her children in fourteenth-century depictions of the liberal arts, the clerk literally becoming what de Bury calls "the nursling of books" (fig. 6). But at the same time she is the cruel mother who wields a birch. The trauma of actual schoolroom learning of Latin was forever inscribed on the bodies of boys. As Karl Morrison observes, "the association of love and inflicted pain, formed in childhood, had its role to play in the formation of adult habits."[29]

The close association between the mother's body and language acquisition in the fourteenth century is suggested by the opening of a Cambridge manuscript of Walter of Bibbesworth's treatise on how to speak French, written for an English noblewoman wanting to teach her children the niceties of the courtly language. The first words are those of the body—head, eyes, lips and reading downwards to the feet. One can imagine from the manuscript layout, with the interlinear English gloss, the child on its mother's knee learning to find the names for the parts of its own body as it is still tied to another (fig. 7). The lost object of the mother's body, around which all fetishism evolves, according to Freudian theory, comes to the surface in chapter 7 of the *Philobiblon* in the account of the transfer of books which Xerxes took from Athens to Persia and which Seleucus brought back again: "O wondrous joy, which you might then see in Athens, when the mother went in triumph to meet her progeny, and again showed the chambers in which they had been nursed to her now aging children! Their old homes were restored to their former inmates . . ." in the beautifully carved shelves of volumes, pleasantly arranged so that "no-one hinders the entrance of another or injures its brother by excessive crowding" (77–79). As opposed to these maternal metaphors of security, in the very first chapter we read of the decay of all things and how "Saturn ceases not to devour the children that he generates" (17). The devouring male body of the father, which tears and destroys what it creates, is here contrasted to the female body that generates offspring to be nurtured and loved.

As well as the good breast focused around oral gratifications, the book later becomes the object of scopic, heterosexual desire. De Bury describes the luxurious parks of volumes in Paris, the paradise of the world with its "delightful libraries, more aromatic than stores of spicery" where "the days seemed ever few for the greatness of our love" (85). The language here uses the topoi of classical Ovidian and Virgilian poetry, the locus amoenus transformed into the page itself. The Bishop's strictly male world opens up here for a moment as he admits that those "of both sexes and of every rank or position who had any kind of association with books could most easily open by their knocking the door of our heart and find a fit resting place in our affection and favour" (95–97). His bibliophilia here becomes more polymorphous, bisexual in its appetites, open to persuasion by either men or women who offer him their flesh in the form of their parchment. Although he states in chapter 8 that he made acquisitions by gift, purchase, or loan, there is evidence that sometimes he gained treasured tomes in less respectable ways, since "we were reported to burn with such desire for books, and especially old ones, that it was more easy for any man to gain our favour by means of books than of money" (83). This remark has led at least one modern and no less misogynistic commentator to state that "the wiles of the collector are as notorious as the wiles of women, and his chief aim is to 'captivate the affection of all' who can get him books."[30]

If books are male through their grammatical gender, their authors, and their voices in the *Philobiblon*, desire for them can only be mediated through the female, through mother or woman, with a gaze that is penetrative and phallic. In chapter 8 de Bury also employs the common metaphor of the hunt for the small animal to describe the books that could not escape his *venatores*, a motif ubiquitous in the bas-de-pages of fourteenth-century manuscripts. I usually interpret such a metaphor as the reader's hunt for truth in the thicket of meanings, but in de Bury's case it becomes a more gendered, voyeuristic hunt for venery (fig. 8).[31] An example of the extreme lengths to which this hunt could go, recorded in the St. Albans Chronicle, is when the bishop took from the Abbot of St. Albans the bribe of four books—a Terence, a Virgil, a Quintilian, and a Jerome, *Contra Rufinum*—as well as the promise of buying thirty-two others for fifty pounds in return for preventing his initiating a royal inquiry into the abbey's mismanagement. Although the angry monks forced him to return some of these volumes, he did not give back an illuminated twelfth-century manuscript of John of Salisbury's works, which bore an inscription calling down anathema on any who should remove the book from the abbey.[32] Clearly the bibliophile's desire took precedence over the book's own magical, threatening voice, a voice de Bury ventriloquizes in the *Philobiblon* but obviously does not fear.

Since he has taken no notice of the voice of the books themselves, he actually projects his own voice onto them, in a transference that is a common psychological strategy of the obsessive identification with the victim of one's obsession. That the books are themselves given a voice is the first startling indication of this ventriloquism, more subtle than that in the fabliaux which give the vagina and arse a mouth, as the flapping folios turn into chattering penetrable and highly gendered objects. Eating was a major metaphor of learning because of the ruminative practices of medieval reading (see, for example, the somatic associations of eating the book in Ezekiel). But here the positive associations of food are contrasted with the negative desires of the other senses, as when in chapter 6 he criticizes the "apocryphal imbecilities" that are not for "the refreshment of souls" but for "pruritum potius aurium auditorum" ("tickling the ears of the listeners").[33] And yet in chapter 5, foodstuffs become the debased reading matter of the clergy "flocks and fleeces, crops and granaries, leeks and pot-herbs, drinks and goblets" (57). As Michel Jeanneret has described in his study of texts and table-manners, "The reader-eater takes possession of the object being read, assimilates this foreign body and makes it part of his own being."[34] According to de Bury, monks prefer the sound of sensual mastication to the *ruminatio* of the *lectio divina*. The hum of the *cursus* itself was a feast for the ears and again reminds one of the vegetable luxuriousness of marginalia in many fourteenth-century manuscripts. Just as twelfth-century monks had, in St. Bernard's words, "read in the marble" those monstrosities carved in the Romanesque cloister, fourteenth-century prelates preferred the more hearty fare of wild game and spices that luxuriated in the images in the margins of their books.

De Bury's major mode of presenting his library uses metaphors, not of bodily orifices and openings, but of familial associations, bonds that it was impossible for him, as a bishop, actually to experience, except illegitimately. When the books speak against the mendicants in chapter 6 they complain of the "three-fold care of superfluities," "of the stomach, of dress, and of houses" which have seduced men from their "paternal care of books" (61). Familial custody rescues parchment from the worldly sin of concupiscence. The Bishop, as father of his flock as well of his books, takes great care of the children entrusted to him but although saving them from the violation of others, he still penetrates them constantly himself and enjoys looking at them as his own personal property.

Having coded the bibliophile's love as the male gaze upon the feminized object, de Bury goes on to position women's real bodies as deeply dangerous to books. Again he uses traditional ideas from traditional misogynist literature, the most commonplace being the wife, about whom the books complain most vociferously, although he adds a strange twist by which the books retain their "secrets" about the evils of the female sex, even from the objects of their animosity, who are too ignorant to understand them. Books, like women's bodies, were often associated with the metaphors of the "secret."

> For our places are seized now by dogs, now by hawks, now by that biped beast whose cohabitation with the clergy was forbidden of old, from which we have always taught our nurslings to flee more than from the asp and cockatrice; wherefore she, always jealous of the love of us, and never to be appeased, at length seeing us in some corner protected only by the web of some dead spider, with a frown abuses and reviles us with bitter words, declaring us alone of all the furniture in the house to be unnecessary, and complaining that we are useless for any household purpose, and advises that we should speedily be converted into rich caps, sendal and silk and twice-dyed purple, robes and furs, wool and linen: and, indeed, not without reason, if she could see our inmost hearts, if she had listened to our secret counsels, if she had read the book of Theophrastus or Valerius, or only heard the twenty-fifth chapter of Ecclesiasticus with understanding ears. (43)

As so often in medieval culture, codes are quickly reversed; one minute de Bury is reviling women and in the next elevating the personified female principle. In chapter 15 "Of the Advantages of the Love of Books," de Bury describes how, "this love called by Greeks philosophy" is a "she" who "as a heavenly dew extinguishes the heats of fleshly vices" (137). Liquid metaphors are often associated with reading as a fountain of cool pleasures rather than hot desires, escaping the feverish body's needs in the frozen bath of textuality. Since the late medieval body and its internal ebbs and flows were literally ruled by the stars, it is also interesting to note that de Bury's excuse for his passion is also partly astrological/humoral and constitutional, for it was "under the aspect of Mercury [I] entertained a blameless pleasure in books" (167). This is a fascinating place where de Bury is analyzing himself, finding an excuse in the medieval temperamental psychology of the "Children of the Planets" tradition, which tied different types of profession, desire, and even body, with those celestial bodies circling above.

Just as astrology focused upon the moment of the conception of the fetus, de Bury is obsessed with the founding moment of writing as a sexual act. He complains in chapter 9 that "The pen of every scribe is now at rest, generations of books no longer succeed each other." Just as French soldiers are unmanned and languishing ("sic eiusdem militia penitus evirata languescit") philosophy in that country is likewise castrated and "lukewarm," referring to the heat of male passion necessary for coitus and therefore human reproduction. Such metaphors were common, as in Nature's famous call for clerics to get down and "plough" the page with their pens in the *Roman de la Rose*. However, de Bury has to be careful in using these old tropes, lest they make the association between book and body too explicit. Standard Aristotelian theories of generation of the period, for example, saw the male providing the form and the female the matter of the fetus. This would make the author's inscription, his word, his seed planted on the female flesh of parchment. So in chapter 16 books are copied and men beget sons so that "the perpetuity of which the individual is by its nature incapable may be secured by the species." Quoting Ecclesiastes 12, "Of making many books there is no end," de Bury argues for textual immortality without the necessity for maternal materiality. This avoidance lies at the heart of his attitude to books.

> For as the bodies of books ["librorum corpora"] seeing that they are formed of a combination of contrary elements, undergo a continual dissolution of their structure, so by the forethought of the clergy a remedy should be found, by means of which the sacred book paying the debt of nature may obtain a natural heir and may raise up like seed to its dead brother, and thus may be verified by that saying of Ecclesiasticus: "His father is dead, and he is as if he were not dead; for he hath left one behind him that is like himself." Thus the transcription of ancient books is as it were the begetting of fresh sons, on whom the office of the father may devolve, lest the commonwealth of books suffer detriment. (147)

Mortifying the Book

Books are bodies also in their vulnerability to disease and death, enduring pains in their backs, their "limbs unstrung by palsy" and their whiteness turned "to dun and yellow." Not only do they suffer from gout but de Bury describes how smoke and dust "have dulled the keenness of our visual rays, and are now infecting our bleared eyes with ophthalmia" (45). These blinded and sick books are surely significant in terms of de Bury's own physical deterioration during the writing of the *Philobiblon*. Although we do not know the nature of what chroniclers described as his "longa infirmitate decoctus," the wailing of the sick volumes are compared to "the two Lazaruses and Job." The epidermal excesses of these two Biblical figures of patient suffering are also iconographically significant in relation to the tears and sores that disfigure parchment, and are another instance of de Bury's visual identification with the objects of his desire. It is only when describing books as victims of violence and subjects of suffering that de Bury ever gets close to the flesh of volumes.

Just as Job knows that his redeemer shall give him eternal life, books await the final day, which comes sooner than expected. In chapter 8, on opportunities for collecting, the bishop relates how he has managed to amass the largest private library in England by resurrecting old volumes. He made discoveries in old aumbries and chests in monasteries: volumes that had "slumbered through long ages in their tombs wake up and are astonished." Rousing these volumes "from their sepulchres," de Bury's metaphor is of the resurrection of the flesh of volumes, flesh that is re-animated by the spirit and where his gaze, equated with that of God at the Last Judgement, literally brings the dead to life. These "long life-less books" eaten by mice and "pierced by the gnawings of the worms," "once clothed in purple and fine linen" (a *vanitas mundi* topos), "now lying in sackcloth and ashes, given up to oblivion, seemed to have become habitations of the moth" (83). The penitent volumes receive their just rewards under the bishop's saving grace. Like a physician among stores of gums and spices, they can then become "the object and the stimulus" of his "affections." He seeks to possess them, "some by gift, others by purchase and some lent to us for a season" (83). From the huge tomes of canon law to the slender quires of "yesterday's sophisms" de Bury's book collection was adopted, like a child is adopted, in a trope of rescue or salvation. Books are freed from being "sold for bondmen and bondwomen and lie as hostages in taverns." Others are rescued from heretical interpretations: "some of our parents have been infected with pestiferous venom" of "Jews, Saracens, heretics and infidels" (47). Textual infection here suggests that the "purity of our race" has been diminished by "compilers, translators and transformers." In de Bury's eyes poor copies are bastards, ruined by compilers, revisers and (worst of all) translators.[35] This eugenics of textual authority sees a heritage distorted by bibliophilic intermarriage, which results in degeneration. There are even imposters among the volumes: "Ah! how often ye pretend that we who are ancient are but lately born, and try to pass us off as sons who are really fathers." In chapter 4 the books' complaints about translation are couched in terms of the loss of nobility through textual fornication, making future generations "wholly degenerate." Likewise, the name of some "wretched stepfather" is attached and sons are "robbed of the name of their true father." De Bury refers to the unauthorized copying of exemplars when he states that they are "born again in Paris based on no affinity of blood."[36] If the mother's milk was fundamental for maintaining the child's learnt self-image, the father's corpse as textual model is the only means of preserving it in perpetuity.

Defiling the Book

As well as intermingling gender, books complain of having to cross class boundaries and face even more ignoble dangers. "Any seamster or cobbler or tailor or artificer of any trade keeps us shut up in prison for the luxurious and wanton pleasures of the clergy ['superfluis et lascivis deliciis clericorum']."[37] Here the mistreatment by the laity is linked with the perverse pleasures of those who should know better, the literate clergy—the very group to which de Bury himself belongs. This anxiety was visualized in luxury books made for wealthy prelates, like the Psalter of Prior Stephen of Derby, which shows uncouth members of the lower orders in the interstices of the letters, and in contrast to the clergy performing the divine office at the center, perverting the pages they hold before them with their gawping mouths and dirty looks (fig. 9).

Another process, in addition to translation, which is even more directly linked to perversion in the *Philobiblon* is manuscript painting. Both are excesses in de Bury's terms. The books complain that "in us the natural use is changed to that which is against nature ['contra naturam'] while we who are the light of faithful souls everywhere fall a prey to painters knowing nought of letters, and entrusted to goldsmiths to become, as though we were not sacred vessels of wisdom, repositories of gold leaf ['repositoria bractearum']."[38] Joining effeminacy with artifice was a standard rhetorical gesture, but the bishop's hint at the most notorious sin against nature—sodomy—has not been discerned in this text before. Decorating the borders of books, with flowers and other small devices, was clearly thought by some to be an effeminization of the text, corrupting truth with painted artifice. From this scholars have argued that the bishop did not collect lavishly illuminated books. Yet not much later he says that he kept at his manors "no small multitude of copyists and scribes, of correctors, binders [and] illuminators" (95), suggesting again that he does not heed the complaint of the books, in light of his own desire. De Bury was writing during a period when richly illuminated manuscripts were being collected by the wealthy prelates and princes of Europe, when the mise-en-page of the book develops from the earlier abstract bar-border and into trellises of naturalistic leaves, lush fruits, male and female bodies and parts of bodies, all growing to be plucked, picked, and eaten from the fleshly pages. These ductile, semi-human, and protean bodies, that are in themselves glosses and that appear in the margins of manuscripts of the period, such as the Gorleston Psalter, made for another leading prelate in fourteenth-century England, simultaneously satirize and arouse desires for illicit penetration.[39]

The anxiety about defilement and corporeality in relation to the book are most strongly expressed in chapter 17 on the bodily handling of books. Here we read that "next to the vestments and vessels dedicated to the Lord's body unclean hands should not touch them." Restored to their "proper places" and "inviolable custody," "they may rejoice in purity while we have them in our hands." Nothing alerts us more to the physical aspect of de Bury's mania for the smell, touch, and feel of skin against skin than the following horrified observations:

> You may happen to see some headstrong youth lazily lounging over his studies, and when the winter's frost is sharp, his nose running from the nipping cold drips down, nor does he think of wiping it with his pocket handkerchief until he has bedewed the book before him with the ugly moisture. Would that he had before him no book, but a cobbler's apron! His nails are stuffed with fetid filth as black as jet, with which he marks any passage that pleases him. He distributes a multitude of straws, which he inserts to stick out in different places, so that the halm may remind him of what his memory cannot retain. These straws, because the book has no stomach to digest them, and no-one takes them out, first distend the book from its wonted closing and at length, being carelessly abandoned to oblivion, go to decay. (157)

The chattering boy eats and even sleeps on the volume, wrinkling and folding the leaves, pressing flowers there in spring, using his "wet and perspiring hands" to turn over the pages. His dusty gloved fingers, fresh from the chase will "hunt line by line through the page" and then in impatience throw the book aside, still open, where it accumulates dust until it "resists the effort to close it" (159). There is enormous emphasis here upon shutting volumes. What alarms the bishop most is the open body of the book penetrable and unprotected, available to the gaze of others. This is why the library, the chained and closed rows of supervised bodies, forms a kind of simulacrum of his own controlled body. He urges that the "smutty scullion reeking from the stewpots does not touch the lily leaves of books" (161), and he asks all scholars to wash their hands before they begin reading. Clean and decent hands would be a benefit to books were it not for the fact that, as he sadly admits, "scabies et pustulae" are also characteristics of the clergy. The psychological association between dirt and death, his fear of the defilement of the virgin vellum, is obvious. But sometimes these bodies actually leave more artful marks:

> But the handling of books is specially to be forbidden to those shameless youths, who as soon as they have learned to form the shapes of letters, straightway, if they have the opportunity, become unhappy commentators, and wherever they find an extra margin about the text, furnish it with monstrous alphabets, or if any other frivolity strikes their fancy, at once their pen begins to write it.[40]

This is not a criticism of the licit manuscript illumination which de Bury had previously criticized as being effeminate, but rather the doodle-like additions of readers that one finds in many fourteenth-century English manuscripts. This book graffiti occurs for example in a law book in Princeton, which no less than three different generations of pseudo-doodlers have added to in their playful reading.[41] "Injuring the usefulness and value of the most beautiful books," what our postmodern sensibilities enjoy as the open and constantly rewritten texture of the always unfinished text, was a shocking sign of promiscuity to the book-loving bishop.

Children, who cannot stop themselves touching (and touching themselves), and the laity, who "look at a book turned upside down just as if it were open in the right way, are utterly unworthy of any communion with books" (161). The voyeur who just likes to look is here projecting his own disgust, the way his body is interpolated into the pages, just like the scruffy schoolboy's, onto the experience of the socially inferior other. The social demarcation of the reader is here at its most extreme. While he says that it "behooves us to guard a book much more carefully than a boot," with reference to an item in the modern fetishist's arsenal, the book is here introjected into de Bury's imaginary, not so much to replace the lost phallus, but rather as a barrier to it. Representing a fear of penetration, a need for virginity and intactness, it seems related to the Christological core, a body that lies at the heart of the *Philobiblon* but which dare not speak its name. This is perhaps where the psychoanalytic concept of the fetish is perhaps not broad enough to encompass the strangeness and the intricate inventiveness of medieval object-relations.

Memorializing the Book

The fetishist often has a larger desire, which involves carrying the fetish beyond death. In concluding these very preliminary remarks about a text that demands much further analysis than I have been able to give it, I want to say something about how this desire is played-out in the final parts of the *Philobiblon*, which deal with de Bury's quest for immortality. Chapter 19 carefully outlines his plans for the foundation of a college or library which would make his books available to a group of Oxford scholars who were the students from his own Durham diocese. He details the duties of the five "keepers" of the books, who shall "swear that they will use the books for no other purpose than inspection and study" (169). The final chapter is more penitential in tone, written probably as the bishop saw the shadows on his book/ body as it began to close: "Time now clamours for us to terminate this treatise which we have composed concerning the love of books ['amore librorum']." Here de Bury even confesses that his desire may "perchance sometimes have been the occasion of some venial negligence, albeit the object of our love is honourable and our intention upright" (175). If the book can save one from death as he had described in chapter 4, in this final chapter he hopes to "live when dead" in the memories of "our future students." This vicarious existence through the next generation's handling of his flesh is the most audacious appropriation by de Bury of the medieval *auctoritas* of the writer. For he hopes for immortality, not as an author himself, but as the lover and collector of other authors. He ends with a prayer that "we may be delivered from the lust of the flesh, that the fear of death may utterly vanish." The body of the dying prelate does not rest in identification with his multitude of books, but rather with the idea of their totality as a library. This is related to the fetishist's desire to "give reality to the image" as Lacan described, or to set up what Freud called a *Denkmal*, a monument that fixes or reinforces the obsession with fetishistic looking through the erection of a substitute effigy. This monument is quite different from the transient and individual foci of fetishistic practice itself, shoes, fur, books, or whatever. It represents, rather, an ideal that cannot be attained in reality.[42]

De Bury's *Denkmal* was to be this library, a monument effacing and simultaneously systematizing his perversion in a larger institutional eternity of textual interpretation and physical interpenetration. It also represents what Jean Baudrillard, in discussing the theory of collecting, has described as the moment when the self-absorption of the collector is "enrolled within some external project or exigency (whether associated with prestige, culture or commerce)." But Baudrillard sees the collector's move towards the world as unable to overcome his independence from it. His endeavor is always a withdrawal into "an all-encompassing object-system . . . synonymous with loneliness," a loneliness evident on every page of the *Philobiblon*. Baudrillard goes on to describe the failed fetishist collector of the twentieth century in terms that might indeed describe de Bury's situation in the fourteenth: "It is because he feels himself alienated or lost within a social discourse whose rules he cannot fathom that the collector is driven to construct an alternative discourse that is for him entirely amenable, insofar as he is the one who dictates its signifiers—the ultimate signifier being, in the final analysis, none other than himself."[43]

Only months after completing his essay in self-signification, Richard de Bury lay in his last death agony at his manor of Auckland. According to contemporary accounts his servants stole all his movable goods and left him totally naked in his bed apart from an undershirt which someone had rudely thrown over him. His end was not that different from the violent treatment suffered by his own volumes, who complain that "the coverings anciently given to us have been torn by violent hands."[44] It is hard to imagine that the old man did not realize that his debts were so great that his bequest could never, in fact, be honored and that his treasured tomes would have to be dispersed rather than go towards founding that great library. Perhaps this is why, during those last painful months, he gave birth to the *Philobiblon*, which presents itself as more than a part-object of his fetishism, more than just another book that ungrateful sons like myself can continue to mistranslate, misinterpret, penetrate, and soil with dirty fingers, to this very day.

Fig. 1.   Avarice with his chest. West Portal of Amiens Cathedral c. 1220.

Fig. 2. The second seal of Richard de Bury, Bishop of Durham, 1335. Durham Cathedral Archives.

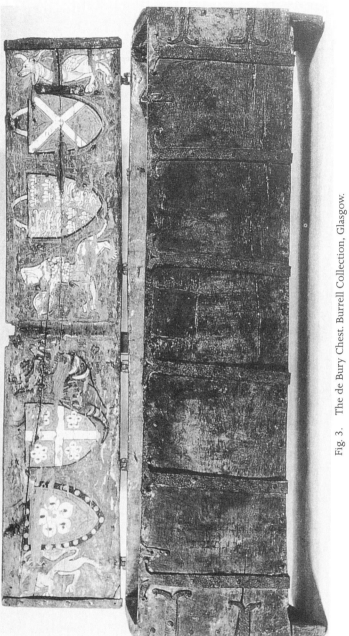

Fig. 3.   The de Bury Chest. Burrell Collection, Glasgow.

Fig. 4.   Monk taking notes on a wax tablet from books in his bed. *Flores Bernardi*, Paris, Bibliothèque Mazarine, MS 753, fol. 9r.

Fig. 5. St. Jerome at his reading wheel passes on scriptural knowledge to a fourteenth-century cleric. Nicholas e Lyra, *Postilla super biblia*, Paris, Bibliothèque Nationale, MS lat. 14247, fol. 1r.

Fig. 6. Grammar's harsh love. Jacques Legrand, *Livre de l'Archiloge Sophie*. Paris, Bibliothèque Nationale, MS fr. 24233, fol. 17v.

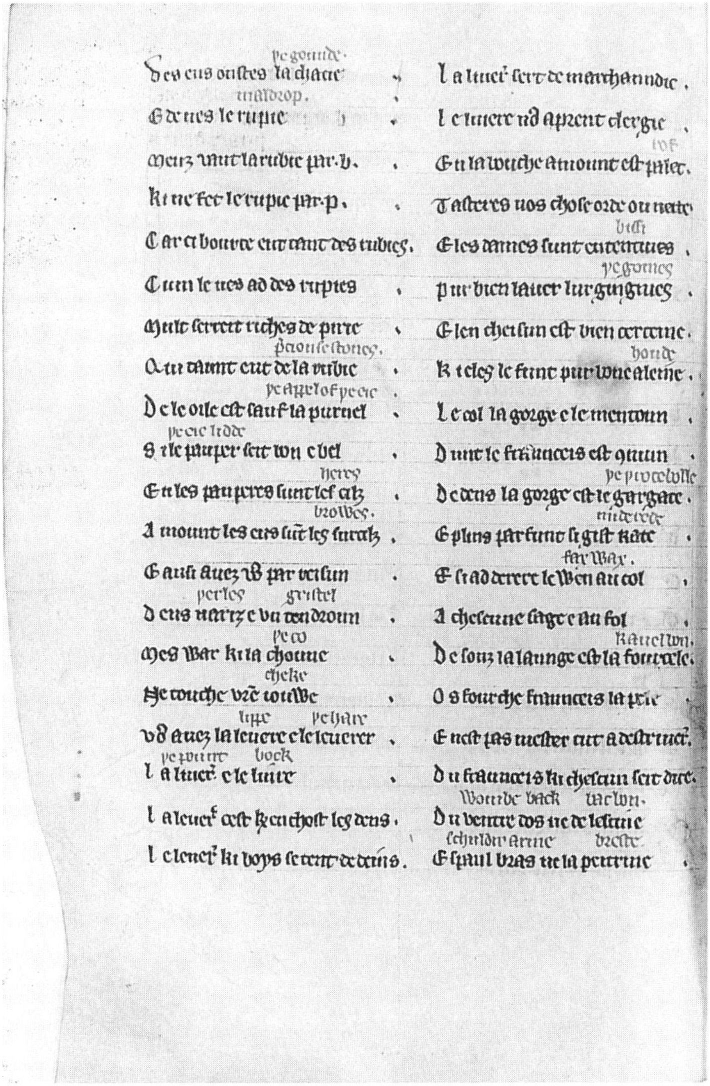

Fig. 7. The mother's body begins the book. Walter of Bibbesworth, *Treatise on How to Speak French*, Cambridge, Cambridge University Library, Gg. 1. 1, fol. 280r.

Fig. 8. The hunt in the text. Grey-Fitzpayn Hours, Cambridge, Fitz-william Museum, MS 242, fol. 29r.

Fig. 9.   Clerical versus lay reading. Psalter of Stephen of Derby, Oxford, Bodleian Library, MS Rawlinson G. 185, fol. 81v.

Notes

1. Richard de Bury, *Philobiblon*, ed. and trans. E. C. Thomas, ed. with a foreword by Michael Maclagan (Oxford: Blackwell, 1960), 13. References to the *Philobiblon* in the text are to this edition. The best critical text is still *Riccardo da Bury, Philobiblon*, ed. Antonio Altamura (Naples: Fausto Fiorentino, 1954). A new, updated, and affordable translation is sorely needed.

2. Frederick Somner Merryweather, *Bibliomania in the Middle Ages*, new and rev. ed. (London: Woodstock Press, 1933), 117. For a history of the printed editions see Maclagan's Introduction to *Philobiblon*, l-liv. This lavish volume itself partakes of the same "book-club" luxury of the "very handsomely printed" editions it so lovingly describes. The male gendering of books and bindings as "handsome" (lii), never "beautiful," is a fascinating and little-researched topic.

3. Thomas Frognall Dibdin, *Bibliomania or Book Madness: A Bibliographical Romance* (London: Chatto and Windus, 1876), 12–13; Merryweather, *Bibliomania*, 119.

4. Gilles Deleuze, *The Logic of Sense* (New York: Columbia University Press, 1990), 304.

5. Susan Stewart, *On Longing: Narratives of the Miniature, the Gigantic, the Souvenir, the Collection* (Baltimore: Johns Hopkins University Press, 1984), 37–38. Jacques Derrida, *Of Grammatology*, trans. Gayatri Chakravorty Spivak (Baltimore: Johns Hopkins University Press, 1976), 15, refers to the great chapter of Ernst R. Curtius, "The Book as Symbol" in *European Literature and the Latin Middle Ages*, trans. Willard R. Trask (New York: Harper Torchbook, 1963), 305–6.

6. Carolyn Dinshaw, *Chaucer's Sexual Poetics* (Madison: University of Wisconsin Press, 1989), 18–21.

7. Richard von Krafft-Ebing, *Psychopathia Sexualis, with Especial Reference to the Antipathic Sexual Instinct: A Medico-Forensic Study*, trans. of the twelfth German edition, rev. ed. by F. J. Rebman (New York: Physicians and Surgeons Book Co., 1929), 241.

8. Robert Stoller, *Perversion: The Erotic Form of Hatred* (New York: Pantheon Books, 1975), 132–74. The crucial texts are by Sigmund Freud: "Fetishism," vol. 21, and "Three Essays on Sexuality," vol. 7, in *The Standard Edition of the Complete Psychological Works of Sigmund Freud*, trans. James Strachey (London: Hogarth Press, 1953–66); but see also Jacques Lacan

and Wladimir Granoff, "Fetishism: The Symbolic, the Imaginary and the Real," in *Perversions*, ed. Sandor Lorand (New York: Random House, 959), 265–90 and Guy Rosolato, "Le fétischisme dont se *dérobe* l'objet," *Nouvelle révue de psychanalyse* 2 (1970): 31. For the application of such theories in medieval studies, see Jean Leclercq, "Modern Psychology and the Interpretation of Medieval Texts," *Speculum* 48 (1973): 476–90.

9. Michel Foucault, *The History of Sexuality: Volume One, An Introduction*, trans. Robert Hurley ([New York: Pantheon, 1978], 58; originally published as *La Volonté de savoir* [Paris: Gallimard, 1976]) drew attention to confession as an early example of sexuality being deployed as power (see also for the public imagery of vice). For the cathedral sculptures of the vices see Michael Camille, *The Gothic Idol: Ideology and Image-Making in Medieval Art* (Cambridge: Cambridge University Press, 1989), 9–11. For "the sexuality of things" see Emily Apter, Introduction to *Fetishism as Cultural Discourse*, ed. Emily Apter and William Pietz (Ithaca and London: Cornell University Press, 1993), 2–3.

10. William Pietz, "The Problem of the Fetish, I," *Res* 9 (Spring 1985): 12–13. See also the useful essays collected in *Fetishism as Cultural Discourse*, ed. Apter and Pietz, especially the Introduction by Apter, pp. 1–13.

11. *Adae Murimuth Continuatio Chronicarum*, ed. Edward Maunde Thompson, Rolls Series 93 (1889): 171. If this is true, this makes his amassing of a library and his book even more psychologically significant.

12. Full accounts of de Bury's life are provided by J. Ghellinck, "Un évêque bibliophile au XIVe siècle," *Révue d'histoire ecclésiastique* 18 (1922): 271–312 and 402–508; and *Révue d'histoire ecclésiastique* 19 (1923): 157–200. See also N. Denholm-Young, "Richard de Bury (1287–1345)," *Transactions of the Royal Historical Society*, n.s., 20 (1937): 135–68, reprinted in his *Collected Papers on Medieval Subjects* (Oxford: Blackwell, 1946), 1–25.

13. Beryl Smalley, *English Friars and Antiquity in the Early Fourteenth Century* (Oxford: Blackwell, 1960), 67.

14. Christopher R. Cheney, "Richard de Bury, Borrower of Books," *Speculum* 48 (1973): 325–28.

15. T. A. Heslop, "The Episcopal Seals of Richard of Bury," in *Medieval Art and Architecture at Durham Cathedral*, British Archaeological Association Conference Transactions, vol. 3 (n.p., 1980), 154–62.

16. The chest is reproduced and described in *The Age of Chivalry: Art in Plantagenet England 1200–1400*, ed. Jonathan Alexander and Paul Binski (London: Royal Academy of Arts, 1987), no. 543, pp. 426–27.

17. See *Philobiblon*, Introduction, xxii.

18. See the entry "*book, whore or vagina*" in Gordon Williams, *A Dictionary of Sexual Language and Imagery in Shakespearean and Stuart Literature* (London: Athlone Press, 1994), 131.

19. Malcolm Parkes, "The Provision of Books," in *Late Medieval Oxford*, ed. J. I. Catto and Ralph Evans, vol. 2 of *The History of the University of Oxford* (Oxford: Clarendon Press, 1984–), 407–83 at 478.

20. This stylistic aspect of the treatise has been studied in detail by Noël Denholm-Young, "The Cursus in England," in *Collected Papers*, 45; it has been related to humanist letter-writing genres by Beryl Smalley, *English Friars and Antiquity*, 69.

21. *Philobiblon*, 107. See Neil W. Gilbert, "Richard de Bury and the 'Quires of Yesterday's Sophisms,'" *Philosophy and Humanism: Renaissance Essays in Honor of Paul Oskar Kristeller*, ed. Edward P. Mahoney (New York: Columbia University Press, 1976), 229–57. For the tradition of associating reading medieval texts with food and drink see the evocative study by Ivan Illich, *In the Vineyard of the Text* (Chicago: University of Chicago Press, 1993), 57–65.

22. Michel Foucault, "Fantasia of the Library," *Language, Counter-Memory, Practice: Selected Essays and Interviews*, ed. with an intro. by Donald F. Bouchard, trans. Donald F. Bouchard and Sherry Simon (Ithaca: Cornell University Press, 1977), 91.

23. These are the remarks of William de Chambre (in James Raine, ed. *Historiae Dunelmensis Scriptores Tres*, Surtees Society 9 [London, 1839], 130) describing a commemorative tablet. See N. D[enholm]-Y[oung], "The Birth of Chronicle," *Bodleian Quarterly Record* 8, no. 80 (1933): 325–28.

24. Daniel Williman, *Bibliothèques ecclésiastiques au temps de la papaute d'Avignon* (Paris: Centre national de la recherche scientifique, 1980–), 1:101. Ghellinck's study of de Bury's library estimates that it contained a total of about 1,500 books (p. 175). For the study of collecting as a phenomenon in the Middle Ages see K. Pomian, *Collectors and Curiosities: Paris and Venice 1500–1800* (Cambridge: Polity Press, 1990) and the useful remarks on medieval collections of things in churches as well as private collections in J. von Schlosser, *Die Kunst- und Wunderkammern der Spatrenaissance: Ein Beitrag zur Geschichte der Sammelwessens* (Leipzig: Klinkhardt und Biermann, 1908), 9–27. The relationship between collecting books and other objects has not been fully explored.

25. Fournival's library at Amiens is described in Sorbonne MS 636, edited by Léopold Delisle, *Le cabinet des manuscrits de la Bibliothèque nationale* (Paris: Imprimerie Nationale, 1868–81), 2:518–35, and studied in the important works of A. Birkenmajer, "La bibliothèque de Richard de Fournival, poète et érudit français du XIIIe siècle," in *Études d'histoire des sciences et de la philosophie au moyen age* (Wroclaw: Zaklad Narodowy im. Ossolinskich, 1970), 170–210, and R. H. Rouse, "Manuscripts Belonging to Richard de Fournival," *Révue d'histoire des textes* 3 (1973): 253–69, who shows that Richard's was not a hypothetical library but an actual collection.

26. Andreas Capellanus, *On Love*, trans. P. G. Walsh (London: Duckworth, 1982), 33.

27. *Philobiblon*, 21. For the psychology of perception in the fourteenth century, see Mary Carruthers, *The Book of Memory: A Study of Memory in Medieval Culture*, rev. ed. (Cambridge: Cambridge University Press, 1992), especially chapter 2 on the neuropsychology of medieval memory.

28. André Green, *On Private Madness* (London: Hogarth Press, 1986), 341–42.

29. For the iconography of Grammar as nourisher and disciplinarian, see Michael Evans, "Allegorical Women and Practical Men: The Iconography of the Artes Reconsidered," in *Medieval Women*, ed. Derek Baker (Oxford: Blackwell, 1978), 310. For the painful aspect of pedagogy and its psychological impact see Karl F. Morrison, "Incentives for Studying the Liberal Arts," in *The Seven Liberal Arts in the Middle Ages*, ed. David L. Wagner (Bloomington: Indiana University Press, 1986), 46; see also Elizabeth Pittenger, "Dispatch Quickly: The Mechanical Reproduction of Pages," *Shakespeare Quarterly* 42 (1991): 389–408. De Bury emphasizes that books teach less painfully than grammar-teachers (*Philobiblon*, 21).

30. *Philobiblon*, 83. Ernest A. Savage, *Old English Libraries: The Making, Collection and Use of Books During the Middle Ages* (Chicago: A. C. McClurg, 1912), 181.

31. *Philobiblon*, 89.

32. This episode is discussed in Cheney, "Richard de Bury, Borrower of Books." For London, British Library, Royal 13. D. IV, see George F. Warner and Julius P. Gilson, *Catalogue of Western Manuscripts in the Old Royal and King's Collection* (London: British Museum, 1921), 2:109–10 and 4:80.

33. *Philobiblon*, 61.

34. M. Jeanneret, *A Feast of Words: Banquets and Table Talk in the Renaissance* (Chicago: University of Chicago Press, 1991), 129, especially "Metaphors of Bibliophagy," 131–39. Many of the classical authorities, such as Seneca, discussed in this study of sixteenth-century food metaphors are also those that the fourteenth-century bishop knew. For the clergy's food see *Philobiblon*, 57.

35. Jan-Dirk Müller, "The Body of the Book: The Media Transition from Manuscript to Print," in *Materialities of Communication*, ed. Hans Ulrich Gumbrecht and K. Ludwig Pfeiffer, trans. William Whobrey (Stanford: Stanford University Press, 1994), 32–44 at 40. For the iconography of the book related to the body see Michael Camille, "The Image and the Self: Unwriting Late Medieval Bodies," in *Framing Medieval Bodies*, ed. Sara Kay and Miri Rubin (Manchester: Manchester University Press, 1994), 62–100.

36. *Philobiblon*, 49. This genealogy of the library is not only a fourteenth-century phenomenon. Walter Benjamin in his famous essay, "Unpacking my Library," *Illuminations*, ed. Hannah Arendt, trans. Harry Zohn (NewYork: Schocken, 1976), 59–64, describes how "a collector's attitude to his possessions stems from an owner's feeling of responsibility towards his property. Thus it is, in the highest sense, the attitude of an heir." Giorgio Agamben also sees a close relation between collecting and fetishism in his *Stanze: Parole et fantasme dans la culture occidentale* (Paris: Éditions Payot, 1992), 71.

37. *Philobiblon*, 47.

38. *Philobiblon*, 51. For the vice *contra naturam* as sodomy, see Vern L. Bullough, "The Sin Against Nature and Homosexuality," in *Sexual Practices and the Medieval Church*, ed. Vern Bullough and James Brundage (Buffalo: Promethius Books, 1982), 64–65. For sodomy as inscribed in the materials of a fourteenth-century Italian manuscript, see Michael Camille, "The Pose of the Queer: Dante's Gaze/Brunetto Latini's Body," (forthcoming in *New Literary History*).

39. For the Gorleston Psalter, see Karl Wentersdorf, "The Symbolic Significance of the 'Figurae Scatalogicae' in Gothic Manuscripts," *Word, Picture and Spectacle*, ed. Clifford Davidson (Kalamazoo: Medieval Institute Publications, 1984), 1–20.

40. *Philobiblon*, 159. In contrast to de Bury's obsessive worries about defilement, the later humanist Erasmus writes that "I consider as lovers of books, not those who keep their books hidden in their store-chests

and never handle them, but those who, by nightly as well as daily use, thumb them, batter them, wear them out, who fill up all the margins with annotations of many kinds"; see *The Correspondence of Erasmus*, ed. R. A. B. Mynors and D. F. S. Thomson, 11 vols. (Toronto: University of Toronto Press, 1974), 1:58.

41. For this manuscript see Michael Camille "In the Margins of the Law: An Illustrated Register of Writs in the Morgan Library," in *England in the Fourteenth Century: Harlaxton Medieval Studies III*, ed. N. Rogers (Stamford: Paul Watkins, 1993), 1–15.

42. M. Masud R. Khan, "The Role of the 'Collated Internal Object' in Perversions," *Alienation in Perversions* (New York: International Universities Press, 1963), 134–38. I also benefitted from reading an essay by Whitney Davis, "The Vision and the Body of Fetishism" (Paper presented at the annual meeting of the College Art Association, Washington, January 1991).

43. Jean Baudrillard, "The System of Collecting," in *The Cultures of Collecting*, ed. John Elsner and Roger Cardinal (Cambridge, MA: Harvard University Press, 1994), 24.

44. These last sad biographical details are recounted in *Adae Murimuth Continuatio Chronicarum*, 171, and Ernest A. Savage, *Old English Libraries*, 179.

CHAPTER THREE

The Courtly Body
and Late Medieval
Literary Culture

Seth Lerer

Notice the copula. I do not say "The Courtly Body *in* Late Medieval Literary Culture," do not concern myself primarily with the formations of courtliness or the literary presentations of the courtier's self in poetry or plays that we have defined as "late medieval." Instead, I am interested in the construction of the courtly body through the reading and reception of late medieval literature: in that nexus of self-absorption and self-fashioning that, I believe, defines the origins of English courtly culture in the first decades of the sixteenth century and, in turn, shapes the environments in which the inheritance of Middle English poetry was read, transmitted, and rewritten. Early Tudor courtly life is, to a large degree, controlled by the paradigms of Chaucer's verse, and the literature of early Tudor courtliness—the allegorical romances of Stephen Hawes, the satiric poetry and drama of John Skelton, and the anonymous, yet popular, verse lessons in the arts of love printed by Wynkyn de Worde, Richard Pynson, and others—often defines its social role through figurations of a body of literature, and a literary body, that is distinctively post-Chaucerian. The work of the courtly author legitimates itself through a metaphorics of corporeal display that is identifiably part of the Middle English literary inheritance. What I wish to argue in this essay is that the formation of the early Tudor courtly body constitutes a critical reception, and rewriting, of a late medieval English corporeal poetics.

I have argued elsewhere that late-fifteenth-century literary culture confronts the corporealized status of the Chaucerian legacy and, in the process, constructs a poetic father or master out of the physical remains, as it were, of his body and his books.[1] Chaucer's own corpus figures prominently as the introductory device throughout the early printings of his works: from the prologue to Caxton's 1478 edition of the *Boece*, with its publication of the Latin epigraph on Chaucer's tomb and the directions to its site in Westminster Abbey, through the sixteenth-century editions of the complete works prefaced by an author portrait and a picture of the poet's tomb.[2] Chaucer is buried, yet remembered; absent from his texts, yet vividly present. The vision of the poet's tomb, and in turn, the representation of the printed book as something of a monument to the inhumed authorial body, defines for English Chaucerians—as much as it defined for Continental Humanist Virgilians and Ovidians—the place where vernacular literary making may be authorized.[3] For the poet Stephen Hawes, one of the most widely-read Chaucerians of the early Tudor period, that nexus of the body and the book becomes the printed volume: a mechanically created monument to literary fame that is presented as immutable as the golden diction in which it is written. Throughout his major publications, from the *Pastime of Pleasure* printed in 1509 through the *Conforte of Louers* printed in 1515, Hawes worked exclusively with Wynkyn de Worde to produce artifacts so that, as in those of Chaucer's typset volumes, the poet's "goodly name/ In prynted bokes/doth remayne in fame."[4]

I would like to reconsider this conception of late medieval authorial self-legitimization through a new look at the forms of bodily display during the first decades of the sixteenth century.

My goal, in the process, is to rehistoricize the post-Chaucerian tradition as an early Tudor cultural phenomenon—to see it not along the teleologies of a development from medieval to Renaissance, but instead, to locate the formations of early Tudor courtly literature as a moment in the history of reception. What is received, I claim, is a poetics of the body: a conception of the act of writing as trespassing in the space between the private and the public. Now, the traditional line on Chaucer's Tudor inheritance—the story propagated by C. S. Lewis, John Stevens, Raymond Southall, H. A. Mason, and others—is that his poetry provided Henry's court with a script for the public life: with the templates for amorous dalliance, courtier performance, and verbal exchange.[5] This is a world of pastime with good company, of stable male and female gender roles, of glitter after the Drab Age of late medieval clerics. Much has, of course, been done to dismantle such a scholarly fantasy, not least by the New Historicist inquiries into the social politics of Tudor literature.[6] But in the current search for textualized histories, the history of certain texts has been effaced, and one goal of my study is to reassess the prominence of Hawes's work in a contemporary courtly literary system and in the cultural transmutation of Chaucerian paradigms to sixteenth-century readers. My central claim is that those paradigms provided not the rules of public but of private life. Chaucer's *Troilus*, Hawes's *Pastime of Pleasure*, and the many early sixteenth-century lyric and narrative works cobbled out of their stanzas, offered models not for pastime with good company but for surreptitions by oneself. These texts write out the narratives of secret correspondence, diplomatic intrigue, and illicit love; they figure forth anxieties about the visualization of the body and the proper codes of physical desire; they thematize the choices offered between personal friendship and public service. They operate in that "nexus of power, sexuality, and inwardness" that has been seen—at least since Stephen Greenblatt's *Renaissance Self-*

Fashioning—as the defining condition of literary culture in the age of Henry VIII.[7]

Hawes's work exemplifies these confrontations of the public courtly body and the private reading self, and in the *Conforte of Louers* the pitfalls of courtier performance script themselves out on the body of a book and on the book of the body. The *Conforte* is a poem about the dangers of illicit desire and the consequences of poetic rivalries and the whims of patronage. Read as a landmark in the tired topography of Chaucerian impersonation—as it almost is—it reeks more of Lydgate than of life, and, indeed, its characteristically self-deprecating prologue sets its literary and political agendas more securely in the nostalgias for Hawes's predecessor poets and the golden age of Henry V than in the courtly realities of his competitors and Henry VIII. But, read in the environment of its contemporary composition and reception, the *Conforte* stands as a complex, troubling assessment of the courtly body and its poetic representation. With its sly barbs against Hawes's more successful courtier poet, John Skelton, it stands as a document of that competitive self-fashioning that, as David Carlson has recently observed, defined the early Tudor coteries of Skelton and Alexander Barclay, Bernard André and Thomas More.[8] Hawes's work provides the lens in which the courtly reader would recover, not just the inheritance of Middle English verse but the intrigues of Henrician literary politics, and for one such reader—the Staffordshire lawyer and minor Tudor confidant Humphrey Wellys—his poetry constitutes the building blocks for a personal response to both that current and past literary history. In Wellys's personal anthology, compiled sometime during the 1530s (now Oxford, Bodleian Library, Rawlinson C. 813), we may observe the makings and unmakings of the courtly self: an act of deeply personal, yet culturally representative, reading and rewriting that, on the pages of his manuscript, traces the tremulations of a very tremulous private body.[9]

From its first lines, the *Conforte* writes itself upon the literary body. After reviewing the accomplishments of Gower, Chaucer, and Lydgate, and after lamenting that Hawes himself has not attained either their own level of literary fame or the level of current political sanction of a "hystoryagraffe nor poete laureate" (20, a clear reference to Henry VII's patronage of Bernard André and John Skelton), the prologue closes with the vision of the dead and buried *auctores* of the vernacular past.[10]

> But syth they are deed / & theyr bodyes layde in chest
> I pray to god to gyue theyr soules good rest.
>
> (27–28)

Here, in an obvious allusion to the Clerk's eulogy of Petrarch in the *Canterbury Tales*, Hawes locates the authorial body in its grave.

> He is now deed and nayled in his cheste;
> I prey to God so yeve his soule reste!
> (*Canterbury Tales*, E 29–30)

The force of this allusion makes the act of literary imitation—whether for Chaucer's Clerk or Hawes himself—a confrontation with the inhumed corporeal form of the *auctor*. Indeed, to be an *auctor* here is to be buried—to be laid or nailed into a "cheste," to be irrevocably removed from the converse of the maker. Hawes's Chaucerian quotation here frames his own book within the body, offering up a paradigm of authorial identity keyed to the various locations of the author's corpus.

If such corporealizations link Hawes to the literary past, they also place him squarely in the political present. Even before these opening lines, the title page of the *Conforte* locates its author in the workings of the courtly body. This is a poem "made and compyled by Steuen Hawes sometyme grome of the honourable chamber of our late souerayne lorde kynge henry ye seuenth."

Hawes had elsewhere been identified as a groom of Henry VII's chamber—for example, in the colophons to the editions of the *Conuersyon of Swerers* and *A Joyfull Meditation*—and this information constitutes a plea for preferment in the new King Henry's court.[11] But it also presents Hawes as a figure in the early history of the privy chamber and, as such, inextricably links poetic service to the service of the royal body. As David Starkey has delineated in great detail, the history of the privy chamber is the history of the king's form. Grooms of the Chamber, Grooms of the Stool, Esquires of the Body—these were the titles granted men who ministered to the king's private functions, and, Starkey argues, it is this new sense of intimacy (especially in Henry VIII's reorganization of his father's administrative structure) that recalibrates the English body politic into a politics of the king's body. Under Henry VIII, these grooms became more than just personal attendants to the king, however. They became the locus of royal trust and, eventually, the minions of his personal diplomacy. As Starkey puts it, the grooms of the privy chamber carried with them "the indefinable charisma of monarchy."[12]

Hawes's status as a former groom reduces whatever monarchical charisma he may have, at least in passing, earlier possessed, and such a public status dovetails with one of the *Conforte's* major private themes: the poet in exile. For the true subject of this poem is not the success of courtiership but its failure. It is a story of books unread, of lost opportunities, transgressive actions, and crushing rivalries. As Alistair Fox has recently argued, the *Conforte's* seemingly deliberate confusion of erotic and political levels of signification is central to Hawes's critique of the courtly poetic career.[13] Fox presses his reading of the poem into a larger claim about Hawes's unrequitable love for Henry VIII's sister, Mary Tudor, and about the political consequences of his early poetry devoted to her. He argues that Mary is the Pucell of the *Pastime of Pleasure*, and he claims that Hawes's whole poetic career encodes an infatuation with a princess far above his station. For Fox,

Hawes's status as a former groom signals a public dismissal, and the *Conforte*, in his aggressively biographical reading, becomes a new plea for preferment and an act of public contrition.

We need not purchase all of Fox's topical allegory to recognize with some assurance that Hawes is preoccupied with one of the central issues of courtier service—social mobility—and that he does present himself as someone painfully, if not fatally, excluded from the workings of the courtly patronage system. But I would argue further that the controlling issue of this poem is not just the status of the courtly poet but the role of illicit desire in what Jonathan Goldberg has recently seen as the role of sexuality in "the formations of courtly literariness."[14] Goldberg defines the story of preferment as the story of exchanging women. Courtly advancement depends on the courtier's ability not just to serve or love, but to dissimulate in both roles. "How are courtly makers made?" he asks, and one answer he offers—and one raised by Hawes in the *Conforte*—is that they are made upon the body.[15] Regardless of the precise topical subtext of this poem, its controlling idiom and imagery challenge the courtly habits of dissimulation. Hawes offers up a courtly body on display: a body readable and knowable; but, as a consequence, a body also subject to the pains, dismemberments, and mutilations of thwarted desire and ambition.

With its repeated emphases on visionary apprehension and its deployment of familiar romance devices of engraved portraits, meaningful mirrors, and significant inscriptions, the *Conforte* narrates a story of the courtly self on permanent display: a story about love that operates somewhere between the dark allegories of "dyuers bokes" made "Full pryueley" and the everyday activities that "all persones . . . openly espyeth" (93–94, 105). Such bodily anxieties, if they have a contemporary topical meaning in the Henrician court, also have a larger literary set of references in Chaucer's poetry. The goodly lady who appears in the narrator's vision often sounds curiously like Pandarus from *Troilus and*

Criseyde. Her string of saws, for example, at lines 148–61, re-calls explicitly Pandarus's advice to the bed-ridden Troilus in Book I. With its rhetorical appositions and its overarching philo-sophical commitment to the mutability of earthly wills, these lines from the *Conforte* expose that tense blend of Boethian advice and courtly pragmatism that distinguishes Pandarus's discourse.[16] Such a discourse, too, governs Hawes's critique of courtiership, as he takes the pandaric condition of the beguiler beguiled and the figurations of the blind man to apply to politics, as well as love. When the poem's narrator approaches one of the many in-scribed texts presented to him on his journey, he finds written there a set of maxims that may be appreciated as a critique of the courtly life itself:

> . . . / it is openly sene
> That many a one / full pryuely dooth wene
> To blynde an other / by crafte and subtylnes
> That ofte blyndeth hym / for all his doublenes.
>
> (361–64)

All the key terms of the *Conforte*'s anxieties are here. The contrast between open appearances and private knowledge, the union of craft and subtlety in construction of a "doublenes" of courtier behavior, and the imagery of moral blindness—all derive from the amicitial paradigms of *Troilus and Criseyde*.[17]

And yet, throughout the *Conforte*, these tidbits of pandaric advice are framed in confessions of great bodily distress. True, Troilus had been ill with love, and Pandarus had come to cure him. But the poem's characters had also been preoccupied with greater pains. Both Troilus and Criseyde, as well as Pandarus, have dreams of arresting physical violence: dreams of dismember-ment and mutilation that, as many recent critics have revealed, stand in for fears of castration and rape.[18] Criseyde's dream of the eagle tearing out her heart (II.925–31), Troilus's nightmare of the boar with its threatening "tuskes grete" (V.1233–46), and

Pandarus's own uneasy and allusive early morning fantasy of Procne and Tereus (II.64–70) all signal a profound set of anxieties about the body of the lover and the friend. In the *Conforte*, Hawes displaces these threats to bodily integrity onto the narrator himself. His own brutal dismemberment resonates with these Chaucerian moments, as they make the narrator into an uneasy blend of Troilan lover and Orphic poet:

> Aboue .xx. woulues / dyde me touse and rent
> Not longe agone / delynge moost shamefully
> That by theyr tuggynge / my lyfe was nere spent.
> (163–65)

This is a literary body that, as Hawes puts it a few lines later, "had but lytell rest" (170), where "subtylte" and "cruelte" (169, 171) are joined as the conceptual and rhyming pairs of courtly anxiety. The lover-poet here is constantly subjected to bodily constraints: his right hand is bound (135), in what is perhaps an allusion to Hawes's own censure at the court, and later on that hand will grab the magic sword: "I felte the hande/of the stele so fyne/Me thought it quaked/the fyngers gan to stretche" (582–83). In the central portion of the poem, Hawes paraphrases Psalm 129, a canticle rich with the imagery of corporeal violence. The poet's courtly enemies now take on the appearance of the enemies of Zion, as Hawes notes how they have "expunged me," "shytte me in a cage," and how "Vpon my backe synners hath fabrysed" (561, 565, 568). Though this was not one of the psalms later transmuted into Thomas Wyatt's painful paraphrases, it clearly articulates that blend of bodily pain and courtly dominance that was a central feature of Henry VIII's control almost from the day of his ascension. What Stephen Greenblatt finds so characteristic of Wyatt's psalmistry—its obsessions with steadfastness in the fact of bodily vulnerability, its transformation of the politics of torture into the poetics of desire, its underlying equation that "power over sexuality produces inwardness"—all distinguish the world of Hawes's *Conforte*.[19] A generation before Wyatt, he exposes the machinery of inspection and discovery that defines the rhetoric of Henrician power. His appositions between openness and privacy resonate, for example, with the testimonies of ambassadorial intrigue phrased by such diplomats as Luiz Carroz (Ferdinand of Spain's emissary to England)[20] and with such theorists as Erasmus, who, in his treatise on letter writing, distilled the figurations of the *vita aulica* into aphoristic form:

> Arrange your facial expression beforehand at home, so that it may be ready for every part of the play and so that not even a glimmer of your true feelings may be revealed in your looks. You must plan your delivery at home, so that your speech suits your looks and the bearing of your whole body suit your feigned speech. These are the rudiments of courtly philosophy, for which no one will be fitted unless he has first wiped away all sense of shame, and leaving his natural expression at home, has put on a mask, as it were.[21]

If Hawes's poem frames the anxiousness of the male body in a world of courtly wills—if it narrates, in other words, the failures of this kind of Erasmian courtier play-acting—it also shares in the early Henrician anxieties about the female form. If the male body is exposed to pain, the woman's body is the object of a powerful desire. Early Tudor poetry is, par excellence, the poetry of the *blazon*, that rhetorical device that catalogues the woman's body parts and, in the process, makes her not so much a sum of those parts but, rather, a collection of free-floating members—corporeal signifiers, as it were, that are the object of the courtly poet's gaze. Hawes is a master of this blazonerie. Though owing much to Chaucer's earlier descriptions of the female form (say, in the presentations of the dead Lady White in the *Book of the Duchess* or in Troilus's fantasy encounters with Criseyde), he goes beyond those of his master in length and detail. Hawesean blazons are, in fact, more akin to the tours de force of contemporary French *rhethoriquers*, and in its dazzling account of Pucelle's body the *Con-*

forte offers a description that could rival anything of Clément Marot.[22] From her forehead "Vnder her orelettes," down through "the vaynes blewe / in her fayre necke well tolde," to her arms, her waist, and her "longe trayne" upon the floor, Pucelle is a creature of fetishized parts (722–48). This is woman as the synechdochic self, a woman broken up, yet also contained in the beauty of her dress. As in his figurations of the male body, Hawes offers up a woman as a *textus*: a body dressed and readable, covered in text and textiles, "knytte," as he puts it, all together (748).

Hawes's anatomizing of the woman's body articulates a central principle of early Renaissance literature: a fetishizing of the body parts into objects of erotic attraction. Such a device, both cultural and poetic, has been defined for the Petrarchan lyric famously by Nancy Vickers, and Lawrence Kritzman has developed this critical interpretation to describe that blend of writing and desire for the later *rhetoriquers*.[23] Though writing on sixteenth-century French literature, Kritzman's remarks explain precisely what I consider the features of Hawesean description:

> In the *blason anatomique* the female body becomes consubstantial with the body of writing; the representation of the woman depicts that of the poet's imaginary projection of the reality of his desire onto an object that is narcissistically subjectivized. . . . What is ostensibly symbolized here is a phenomenology of desire that entails a dismemberment of the female body, one that conjures up detached body parts or fetishized objects, whose wholeness is entirely phantasmatic. (97, 99)

What is, in Kritzman's phrase, "entirely phantasmatic" in the *Conforte* is not just the wholeness of the woman's body but the wholeness of a body politic and the unity of courtly life. The poem takes the corporeal imagery of the Chaucerian legacy and textures it through the violence and desire of the early Henrician court. It presents courtly writing not as normative and faithful, but as transgressive and seditious, while presenting—in however adumbrated form—a form of male desire that crosses boundaries of class and literary decorum. The *Conforte* presents, in other words, the dark alternative to the brightly lit theatrics of Henrician performance.

To this point, I have argued for a pattern of bodily representation in the *Conforte*: a pattern of figurations that define the courtly self as something of a body on display, caught between openness and priviness. This tension, I believe, is subtly coded, too, in a complex set of wordplays on the titles of Hawes's own works: wordplays that make the body of the author inextricably associated with the body of his work and, in the process, make him into something of a living version of the authorial bodies buried in their chests. One of the key themes of the *Conforte* is the reading and reception, not just of Chaucer and his heirs, but of Hawes's own *Pastime of Pleasure*, and from the very first lines of the poem, Hawes creates a complex structure of self-reference that puns on the titles of both of these works. The "gentyll poetes" to whom he appeals in line 1 are themselves writers of "fables and storyes" that are "pastymes pleasaunt / To lordes and ladyes" (8–9). Such pastimes constitute the currency of public courtiership, and throughout her moral lectures, Hawes's visionary tutorial lady plays on the idea of the "pleasure" courtly books in general, and "youre bokes" in particular may generate (193, 191).[24] Before she departs, she enjoins the poet:

> *Passe* ye *tyme* here / accordynge to your lykynge
> It may fortune / your lady of excellence
> wyll *pass* her *tyme* here / soon by walkynkge.
> > (247–49, emphases mine)

And when she leaves, the poem's narrator laments:

> My herte doth blede / now al totorne and rent
> For lacke of *conforte* / my herte is almost spent

O meruelous fortune / whiche hast in loue me brought
Where is my *conforte* / that I so longe haue sought.

(256–59, emphases mine)

These lines echo precisely the iterations of the previous stanza. By repeating passe . . . *tyme* and *conforte* in exactly the same positions—in alternating lines, with both terms placed before the marked caesura—Hawes brings the two terms together not so much as moral or sensory conditions but as titles of his books. The "conforte" that is sought is to be found in the making of the *Conforte of Louers* itself.

Such bibliopsychiatry, as I would term it, is central to the Hawesean project. As he avers only four stanzas later:

Two thynges me conforte / euer in pryncypall
The fyrst be bokes / made in antyquyte
By Gower and Chauncers / poetes rethorycall
And Lydgate eke / by good auctoryte.

(281–84)

Here, in an obvious return to the literary historiography of the poem's prologue, Hawes makes the act of reading more than just a "pastyme pleasaunt," but a "conforte": in other words, not an activity of public courtly life, not an activity performed by "lordes and ladyes," but rather one of private meditation performed by the author alone. So, too, are books an act of "conforte" in the second point he raises. Hawes's narrator looks forward to those inscribed texts set in the walls or signs along his journey. "Letters for my lady"; "letters for me"; all these are "Agreynge well vnto my bokes all" (291–93). Books and letters are the source of health: the maintenance of the intact private body depends on the reading and writing of texts. "Conforte," in this vocabulary of lisible health, comes to mean quite explicitly the ways in which the courtly body privatizes itself through the act of reading. And yet, not all writers may be granted such a gift.

As Hawes says later in the poem, "Many one wryteth trouthe / yet conforte hath he none" (558).

"Conforte" and "pastime" are the two poles of the courtly self and the two ways of reading and writing in courtly society. As Hawes puts it again, the courtly lover woefully seeks out "only suche pastyme / here for to repayre," and must ask, "Where is my conforte / where is my lady fayre" (627–28). Where, indeed? The narrator becomes progressively a creature of his own texts: his lady is "fayrest and moost swete / In all my bokes," he notes how she greets "Also my bokes full pryuely," and he concludes, "The more I wryte the more my teeres dystyll" (633, 636, 643). Allusions continue to build as Hawes concatenates these terms. Finally, when La Belle Pucelle appears, she explains to the lover-narrator, and to his reader, just what these cryptic references mean. The lover seeks her "swete conforte" (784), and she responds:

> Of late I sawe aboke [sic] of your makynge
> Called the pastyme of pleasure / whiche is wondrous.
> (785–86)

Her remark here is of a piece with the encounters of Hawes's hero of the *Pastime* itself, Grande Amoure, as he comes upon visions of graven scriptures. She sees this book as if it were an artifact, and like Grande Amoure she conflates its physical journeys and its verbal pathways. "I redde there all your passage daungerous" (789), she notes, in an ambiguous allusion to the possible censurable passages Hawes had written and / or to the dangerous passage of his fictional hero. At such a moment, Hawes is inseparable both from his literary personae and his bibliographical productions. The body is the book.

Finally, at the poem's end, when the lover awakes from his literary dream and seeks to take up the pen and write it down, Hawes turns again to his own works. "Go lytell treatyse," he announces (932), in an obvious allusion to the close of *Troilus and*

Criseyde. And yet, what Hawes's own book seeks submission to are not the canons of a classical poetics. This is not a text that will kiss the steps of Virgil, Ovid, Homer, Lucan, and Statius; not a book that, as with Chaucer's, will be submitted for the correction of such learned friends as Gower and Strode. This is, instead, a book that has survived its rivals and its author's exiles. It is a book that has been made in spite of courtly dismissal, in spite of the barbed satires of his literary rivals and the "snares and nettes" of courtly intrigue. Rather, it is a book that goads its reader to return to Hawes's own body of work. It is an envoy that beseeches readers, "From daye to daye theyr pastyme to attende" (937). Not only are these ladies to appreciate the workings of this author, they are enjoined to return to Hawes's signature text, the *Pastime of Pleasure.* To attend their pastime means to reread his book, now through the lens of the apologetics of the *Conforte* and the explanations of La Belle Pucelle.

The Pastimes of Humphrey Wellys

To attend to the *Pastime* is precisely what Humphrey Wellys has done. Many of the poems in his manuscript are grounded in the texts and idioms of Hawes's work. Four of his longest poems are centos cobbled out of the *Pastime of Pleasure,* and one is similarly put together out of stanzas from the *Conforte of Louers.* Even in those texts not drawn from Hawes's writings—for example, the cento put together out of nine stanzas of *Troilus and Criseyde,* and the shorter poems pieced together out of lines and phrases from Lydgate—there is a distinctively Hawesean feel to their verbal texture.[25] Wellys often changes individual words, phrases, or whole lines to bring out the imagery of visualization, engraving, printing, and embossing that had defined Hawes's amatory epistemology.[26] Moreover, Wellys's poems often transform longer narratives into short bills of love. The verse epistle is his standard literary mode here, and he draws explicitly on the elaborate presentations of love letters and sealed documents in Hawes's narratives in order to construct a volume that, when read in sequence, comes to stand as something of a book of intercepted letters. But if Wellys seems to read the legacy of Middle English literature through the scrim of Hawesean allegory, he also reads his Hawes—and for that matter Chaucer, Lydgate, Skelton, and other nameless poetasters—from behind the curtain of contemporary early Tudor politics. This volume is replete with political satire and seditious prophecy. It offers poems about named and known courtiers, as well as pieces located in the topical environment of Wellys's own Staffordshire family romances. Central to this compilation is the yoking together of love and politics: this powerful, potentially transgressive association of amorous intrigue and courtly surreption. Wellys's anthology offers compelling testimony to the construction of the courtly body through the figurations of a literary past.

From its opening items, Wellys's manuscript articulates these anxieties about the place of public bodies in the private missives of amorous exchange. Its first poem is a Hawesean bill of complaint beseeching the recipient, in lines adapted from the *Pastime of Pleasure*, "to gyffe audyence" to the love letter. The lover is constrained by love, "fetteryd" by her beauty, and this image of imprisonment sustains the second poem in the manuscript. Here, in an odd conflation of Promethian legend and Criseydean erotic dream, the narrator imagines himself a prisoner, taken to a beautiful bower where a "bryde"—read either "bird" or "bride"—"wholly fro me my harte hathe take" (2.6). This is a poem of the riven and the fettered body, a poem that defines the enticements not just of beholding the beloved object but of reading the poetry of erotic desire. So, too, is poem 13 in the manuscript, a compilation drawn from stanzas of the *Pastime of Pleasure* and *Comfort of Lovers*. "Regarde and see," it opens, and what we are left to see are both the lover's letter and his beloved's form. Out of the over five thousand lines of the *Pastime*, Wellys has found the most explicit descriptions of the lady's body and has arranged his borrowed stanzas into a trajectory of amatory gazing. The reader moves from the lady's head, through her neck and arms, right down to

> hur pappys were ronde and ther to ryght praytye
> hur armys sclender and of goodly bodye
> hur fyngers smale and þerto ryght longe
> whyt as mylke with blewe vaynes amonge.
>
> (13.123–26)

Such fascinations with the female form—what Kritzman calls the "architecture of the breast" (p. 99)—had already been revealed early in the manuscript, in item number 4, where Wellys transcribes (uniquely) a late Middle English poem on the idealized woman. Again, the catalogue of body parts concludes with hands and breasts:

> hur fyngers be bothe large and longe
> with pappes round as any ball
> no thyng me thynke on hur ys wronge
> hur medyll ys both gaunte and small.
>
> (4.17–20)

In this earlier poem, the lady "hathe my harte" (4.21). But in the Hawes cento, she is "engrauyd" in "my mynde" (13.127). This image of engraving, central to Hawes's literary project, makes the body and the book inseparable. It gives us, in Wellys's private revision, a poem that not only addresses body parts in fetishized or disembodied form; it makes them texts engraved, places them in the ambience of amatory writing—that is, in the inscriptive processes that make the delectations of the hand the cuttings into memory.

In the environs of such cutting, bodies become texts, and the poem becomes a letter written out of fear of discovery and shame. Its narrator relies on trusted friends and readers, recog-

nizes the dangers of being caught, and at the poem's close locates
the transgressions of desire squarely in the public world of imperial England:

> Thys fare ye well þer ys no more to Sey
> vnder my signett yn þe courte Inperyall
> of Aperell þe nyen and twenty day
> I closyd thys lettur and to me dyd call
> desyre my frend Soo dere and espetyall
> cummandyng hym as fast as he myght
> To my swete lady to take ytt full ryght.
>
> (13.162–68)

Wellys's revisions of the stanza are both striking and deliberate.
In the *Pastime of Pleasure*, these lines sustain the classicizing fantasy
of Grande Amoure's desire. They narrate not the sending but the
reading of the missive, and the call is not to the knowing friend
but to the distant Cupid.

> And fare ye well there is no more to say
> Vnder our sygnet in our courte ryall
> Of Septembre the two and twenty day
> She closed the letter and to her dyde call
> Cupyde her sone so dere and specyall
> Commaundynge hym as fast as he myght
> To labell pucell for to take his flyght.
>
> (*Pastime*, 4084–90)

At one level, the author of Wellys's poem simply has recast
these lines to make them consistent with his male speaker; he has
elided the classical reference and changed the date, perhaps, as
the poem's editors suggest, to adapt Hawes's poem "for a particular occasion."[27] But there is more at work here than the simple
changes in the topicality of courtly verse. The poem in the Wellys
anthology sends the letter under the signet of the "court In-
peryall," a reference clearly to the idea of the Henrician court as

the seat of an Empire. Indeed, the imperializing of the Henrician court was part and parcel of Cromwell's articulation of a royal supremacy—the break with Rome, the first divorce, and in 1533, the averral (in the Act in Restraint of Appeals) that "this realm of England is an Empire."[28]

This is a poem, now, that takes place in the specific environments of Henrician power and Cromwellian surveillance. As Edward Wilson has shown, in a study of the topical allusions throughout the anthology, Wellys had close ties to the Chatwyn family of Staffordshire (he married the daughter of William Chatwyn, a sometime member of the court of Henry VIII and later court Escheator), and several of the poems in the manuscript on specifically courtly topics may have derived from exemplars in Chatwyn family manuscripts.[29] Poems on the deaths of Sir Gryffyth ap Ryse and Edward, Duke of Buckingham, as well as the extract from Skelton's *Why Come Ye Nat to Courte*, point to the courtly infightings of the early 1520s, while the fruition dates of the political prophecies illustrate some familiarity with political events of the first half of the 1530s. With such connections, Wellys himself would have to have been wary of his recusant sentiments. His transcription of prophecies against the King would have been just the kind of treasonous action that local acquaintances informed against and which the Parliamentary acts of the late 1530s and early 1540s were designed to legislate against. His writing, and then crossing out, of the word "pope" in several of the poems exemplify what G. R. Elton has characterized as "sedition or disaffection short of treason, . . . the sort of resistance manifested in failure to erase the pope's name from books."[30] And Wellys's own encrypted statement of possession at the close of the manuscript preserves precisely the kinds of "cypheringe" that Henry VIII's acts defined as treasonous.[31] Finally, the inventory of Wellys's will—with its record of "a settel to laye bokes in," and its account of "certen bokes" presented under the heading of "In the studye"—locates his reading matter, and as Wilson has suggested this very manuscript itself, in the enclosures of the private space of reading: in the "studye," a place of secretive withdrawal, and in the "settle," a bench with a locker for secreting books.[32]

The privacies and surreptitions that control this manuscript's externals, and that are revealed in its familial coterie allusions and its defining accouterments of secrecy, encryption, and withdrawal, become the subject of the poetry it offers. Throughout, love is a secret and a surreptitious thing. "Vnto you I nede nott to wryte my name," announces one of the verse letters, and another claims:

> from whens ytt cumethe ytt hath no name
> and whydder ytt shall yt sayethe þe same
> Then passe forthe letter thorow3 þis prese
> and save þi mastur shameles.
>
> (47.65–68)

These are the secret correspondences of unnamed lovers, far different from the signed missives of the "Litera Troili" and "Litera Criseydis" of Chaucer's poem, and different, too, from the specific recipients of the Chaucerian adaptations of the Devonshire Manuscript—where Criseyde's name is omitted from certain stanzas in order for Mary Shelton's name to be inserted.[33] In this environment of anonymity, in a world of secretive unsigned missives and potentially dangerous encounters, the logic of sense impression takes on a new energy. To imprint in the mind—the language of Chaucerian impression and Lydgatean mnemonics filtered through the imagistic obsessions of Hawes—becomes one of the key tropes of these poems. What is inscribed, imprinted, or engraved, though, are not names but forms; not identifiable persons as such but the bodies of the lovers. Hearts and minds, too, are locked up: set deeply away in the recesses of the memory:

> my loue ys lockyd vnder your lace
> my body ys bereyd withyn your bowere.
>
> (34.15–16)

And yet, the lover is not simply a prisoner, but I believe, more akin to one of the seditious books secreted in the settle of the study. As poem 45 puts it, announcing the injunction "prynte þis yn your mynde,"

> for yn your confydence my worde I haue closyde
> bothe locke and kay ye haue yn your gourernance
> and to yow my mynde I haue sayllyde
> Of very pety exyle me nott owt of remembrance.
>
> (45.7–10)

The writer's word is locked up, much like a book closed in the clasps of binding or hidden under the lock and key of the *arca libraria*. Closed in the lover's remembrance, the writer's words now take on something of the status of Chaucer's "olde bookes" which, in the well known equation from the Prologue to the *Legend of Good Women*, are the "keys to remembrance."

In this complex topical environment, we may return to Wellys's Hawesean cento to see its blend of fact and fiction as reflecting on the writer's own anxieties about his body and his book. This is a poem, now, that, at its close relies on trusted friends and secret lovers for its successful transmission—and indeed, for the avoidance of the letter writer's own discovery. In the manuscript, there is a "finis" after these last lines, and a phrase appropriated from the motto of the Order of the Garter: "Si troue Soit hony Soit qui mal y pense" ("If this is discovered, evil to him who evil thinks"). I agree with the manuscript's most recent editors that there "seems to be no special allusion to the Garter motto" here.[34] But it is far more complicated than, as they claim, a simple injunction to secrecy. The meaning of this exhortation lies both inside and outside its fiction. On the one hand, we may take this motto as inscribed on the closed cover of the letter. Its injunction refers to the fear of interception, and as such, it sustains the fiction of an epistle surreptitiously delivered by a knowing friend. But on the other hand, the motto speaks directly to the governing concerns of Wellys's book. It is of a piece with Wellys's own encrypted *ex libris* to the volume. Written in a letter substitution code on fol. 98v are these lines, decoded as follows:

> homffrey Wellis est possesor huius libri
> pertinet liber iste ad me cognomine Wellis
> si unquam perdatur homfrido Restitutum sit.

This mark of ownership has, since its recent discovery, been largely understood to be just that: a statement of the owner's name and, in the words of Edward Wilson, a commentary on the owner's "touching faith in human nature that a finder would not only return the book but would decipher the inscription in order to do so."[35] But there is little faith in human nature, touching or otherwise, behind the coded privacies of Wellys's volume. What Wellys has done here is inscribe himself into the fictions of epistolary writing and return that shape his manuscript. He has, in essence, written out his own assembly of intercepted letters, and his version of the Garter motto offers an illuminating gloss on early Tudor contexts for defining the tensions between private desire and public shame in the construction of the male reader. It signals not a pleasure in the text but almost an embarrassment at fantasy: a vision of the reader now subjected not only to the judgment of an imaginary woman but to the censure of a judging public.

Love is a secret, surreptitious, and suspicious thing, and what characterizes the sequences of verse epistles in this manuscript, and what distinguishes it from other superficially similar assemblies such as the Devonshire and the Bannatyne Manuscripts, is this tension between discovery and secrecy, naming and anonymity. Certain texts seem to revel in the named announcements of local, historical, or courtly personages, defining a coterie of circulation; others are motivated by the self-effacements of a writer who would dare not sign a name, where the received conventions of vernacular versemaking offer letters of familiar, muted generalities. Wellys's manuscript arranges these various essays in identity to construct sequences of letters surreptitiously discerned; to read his *compilatio* is, in a controlling and perhaps disturbing way, to share in the transgressions of the man who reads the man who writes as woman.

For Wellys, as for the early Tudor reader generally, the textbook of such disturbances is *Troilus and Criseyde*, a work that offers in its heroine a male construction of a woman writing, read by other men.[36] With her tentative, resisting gestures of epistolary response, Criseyde enacts a letter-writing tease, a plea for tutelage in the arts of epistolary seduction from a teacher who is himself a model of transgressive lection. To Pandarus's exhortations to compose a letter, she avers "this is the firste lettre / That evere I wroot" (II.1213–14), and the Chaucerian narrator, himself eavesdropping on a scene of private composition, finds her all alone in her "closet" where she writes (II.1215–18). By Book V, Criseyde has apparently learned enough of the conventions of letter writing that she can respond effectively to Troilus's missives; and by Book V, too, the narrator is no longer content with presenting paraphrases of the contents of the lovers' correspondence. The "Litera Troili" and the "Litera Criseydis" remain the earliest examples of epistolary fiction in English poetry, and they have long been appreciated for their controlled manipulations of the social practice of the letter. But in the structure of the poem as a whole, they complete a narrative of texts and their reception that began, not with the missives of the hero but the fictions of a female. At the beginning of the poem, Pandarus had framed his counseling of Troilus around his own, interested misreading of Oenone's letter to Paris drawn from Ovid's *Heroides*

(I.652–55); and at its close, the Chaucerian narrator speaks, in what some have taken as the poet's proper persona, to his intended readers, Gower and Strode, sending off his "little book" for their "correccioun."

In *Troilus and Criseyde* the composition and reception of love letters are those moments when we see the lovers, and their handlers, at their most transgressive. Each letter read and written crosses boundaries of literate ability, social decorum, or authorial intent. An imaginary *Heroid* that becomes a real letter; a set of texts composed by the uninitiated or the incompetent; and a long poem that, at its conclusion, offers itself as a document submitted for review—all come together to estrange the social practice of the letter from the literary transmutations of the art. "Th'entente is al, and nat the lettres space" (V.1630), Criseyde announced in closing her last letter, and with this remark she raises questions about just what is the "lettres space"—what is the proper space of letter writing; what is both appropriate and inappropriate for the personal missive, and for that matter, just how can the brief space of folded paper contain all the feelings of the writer.

> I dar nat, ther I am, wel lettres make,
> Ne nevere yet ne koude I wel endite.
> Ek gret effect men write in place lite.
> (V.1627–29, emphasis mine)

The logic of Criseydean epistolarity centers on the impediments to self-expression posed by male-defined epistolary form. To write letters as a woman is—as she herself and Oenone could testify—by nature to be misread by men.

For Humphrey Wellys, all women are potentially Criseyde. "Womans sayinges trust noot to trulye" (57.16); "doo nott euer beleve the womans compleynte . . . harlottes can collour bothe gloyse and paynt" (57.23, 25). Wantonness, harlotry, deception, elusiveness—all fit the women of these texts, as in the poem with the refrain line "She þat hathe a wantan eye" (21) or in the prose piece distinguishing between a harlot, a hunter, and a whore (29). These are not simply the received tropes of a generalized antifeminism, but a language specifically linked to Chaucer's heroine. It is a language that descends directly from the portrait of her limned by Lydgate; by the references to her in the fifteenth-century *Chance of the Dice* and the *Pastime of Pleasure*; and, of course, by Henryson's *Testament of Cressid*, a work that would have been widely available to Tudor readers in its publication in Thynne's 1532 edition of Chaucer's *Works*. This is the fickle Criseyde, the exemplar of women who are, in the words of Hawes's Godfrey Gobelieve in the *Pastime of Pleasure*, "so subtyll and so false of kynde / There can no man wade beyonde theyr mynde" (3568–69). Such a creature, to continue Hawes's paradigm, is not just adventitious or duplicitous, but also surreptitiously observed, as for example, when Godfrey, a little further on, describes Aristotle's desire:

> For to haue remedy of his sore sekenes
> Whan he her spyed ryght secrete alone
> Vnto her he wente and made all his mone.
>
> (3579–81)

This is precisely the recalibration of the Troilan dilemma that informs Wellys's stance: the woman, now, as creature surreptitiously observed; the woman who potentially would control the man; the woman who, while loving in private is humiliating in public. As Godfrey finishes his story:

> And so a brydle she put in his mouthe
> Vpon his backe she rode bothe northe and southe
> Aboute a chambre as some cherkes [sic] wene
> Of many persones it was openly sene.
>
> (3606–9)

Now, it is neither Troilus nor Diomede who would lead Criseyde by the bridle, as in Chaucer's poem, but this nameless woman

who would turn philosophers into horses and reveal the privy
power-plays of the beloved's chamber to the many in the open.

This is, it seems to me, the context of Chaucerian reception
that defines Wellys's transcriptions of women at their most vulgar
and humiliating. When they are not the creatures of male delectation, they are powerful insulters of the male body. When they
write their own letters of love and friendship to each other, they
dismantle the male body into its scatologized, if not castrated,
private parts, and one of the most powerful of such articulations
of female-female intimacy in the manuscript—indeed, I think in
all of early sixteenth-century verse—is item seven in the manuscript, titled "A lettre sende by on yonge woman to anoder,
which aforetyme were ffellowes togeder." Here, we find not the
courtly rhetoric of female love, nor do we find the finely-tuned
elaborate stanza patterns of the Chaucerian and Lydgatean inheritance. Instead, the reader is subjected to rough couplets and
rough intimacies. Traditionally associated with the genre of Good
Gossips or Alewife poetry of late medieval England, this poem
raises questions central to the construction of the female epistolary persona and the surreptitious male reader. It is a poem full
of local detail, yet also one rich with broader literary implications. Its importance lies not simply in the family intrigues of the
Staffordshire inhabitants it names, but more pointedly in the historical conundrums of the man who reads—or even intercepts—
the writings of the woman.[37]

My loving, ffrende, amorous bune,
I cum ambelyng to you by the same tokyn
That you and I haue be togeder,
And settyn by the ffire in colde wether,
And wyth vs noo moo but our Gullett,
Wyth all the knakes in hur buggett;   'trifles in her bag'
Hur trumpett and hur merye songe
Nowe ffor to here, I thinke itt longe.

Come amble me to hur, I you praye,
And to Agnes Irpe as bright as daye.
I wolde you were here to lokke our gates,
Butt alas itt ys ffare to the jakes.
Ffarewell, ffaire Agnes Blakamoure,
I wolde I hadde you here in stoore,
Ffor you wolde come with all your harte.
Ffarewell, ffarewell, my ladye darke.
Commande me to Wyllyam, I you desyre,
And praye hym to *wyshe vs* some of his ffyre,   'lead us to'
Ffor we haue non butt a coole or a stykke,
And soo we dryve awaye the *weke*.   'weak' or 'week'
And commande me also to the roughe Hollye
That turnethe itt ofte into Godes bodye,   [i.e., bread; in
And to all your oder ffelowes besyde   the Mass]
As well as I hadde ther names discryed.
And praye John Cossall to be goode and kynde,
Ffor the nexte yere he wyl be blynde.
And bydde *Humffrey* doo hym noo shrowed turne, [Wellys?]
For then Sir John muste hym *wor[n]e*.   'restrain'?
Ande commande me to Thomson, that talle man,
Whiche shulde have a *lather* to pisse in a can;   'ladder'
And also to Nicholas with the blake berde,
On whome to loke itt makes me a-fferde.
My vncle3 and my aunte be merye and glade.
And, thankes be to God, I am nott sadde,
And Christoffer, your ffrende, ys off good cheere
And many tymes he wissheth hym ther.
Ffaire tokens I wolde haue sende,
Butt I lakked money ffor to spende.
And thys, ffare you well, this goode Newe Yere
I pray you be merye and off good cheere;
And, ffor the love of swete Seynt Denys,
Att thys my letter thinke noo vnkyndnes,

Ffor to make you all merye I doo ryme,
And nowe to leave I thinke itt tyme.
Att nyne off the clokke thys was wrytten;
I wolde you were all *beshetyn*.   'shit upon'

Rhetorically, this poem seems to violate all the conventions
of formal epistolary discourse set out in the literary models
of Criseydean writing and the many manuals of *dictamen* pro-
liferating in the fifteenth and sixteenth centuries. From its first
line, it establishes a personal relationship between the women
that exceeds conventional amity. It begins, "My loving ffrende,
amorous bune," and later addresses its recipient as "my ladye
darke" (15). The anonymities of writer and reader contrast with
the proliferation of the names in this text, so many "names discryed" that scholars have been able to reconstruct the precise
social ambiance in which it must have circulated among the
Wellys and other families of Staffordshire of the early 1530s.[38]
But the whole point of this missive lies in the contrast between
the identified circle of locals and the unidentified correspon-
dents. Writer and reader stand as anonymous girls in a world
of named, parental and authoritative figures. And while it is
quite pointed in its dating ("Newe Yere") and even its timing
of composition, its concluding lines confirm the correspon-
dents in a playful mockery of social and epistolary decorum
(42–46).

This is a letter that just barely skirts the line between *amor* and
amicitia, between the everyday conventions of epistolary friendship and the innuendoes of intimacy. Who is this "lady darke"
and why is she unnamed? What is the force of the scatology that
closes the letter, and for that matter, of the couplet in the middle
of the poem: "I wolde you were here to lokke our gates, /Butt
alas itt ys ffare to the jakes" (11–12)? And just who is the "amorous bune"? Lexicographically a puzzle, *bune* is a proper name to
Edward Wilson, who confesses in his study of the manuscript:

"not recognized by previous editors as a surname, but I have not identified her."[39] The editors of the recently published edition of the *Welles Anthology* are similarly baffled, and reduced to finding in the OED a meaning "squirrel" and conjecturing a term of endearment. But we need no great proficiency in lexicography or onomastics to see *bune* as just what it appears to be. The OED, in fact, does define *Bun* in northern dialect as "the tail of a hare, also transf. to human beings," and the *Dictionary of the Older Scottish Tongue* concurs (and offers *bune* as an alternative spelling). Both cite a quotation from the Scots poet Sir David Lyndsay, c.1538, contemporary with Wellys's poem: "I lauch best to se ane Nwn, / Gar beir hir taill abouve hir bwn." *Bune* means "buns," and this expression of anatomical intimacy is on a par with the poem's overarching preoccupation with the scatologized body: for example, the use of the familiar Tudor sexual innuendoes of horsemanship in line 9, "come amble me to hur, I you praye"; the blunt insult about Thomson, "that talle man / Whiche shulde have a lather to pisse in a can" (29–30); the concluding wish to shit upon all those named in the letter; and what I believe to be the innuendoes of lines 11 ("have in store"), 18 (the fire of Wyllyam), and perhaps the puns on the name Gullet (5) and rough holly (21).

This is a poem that does not simply violate social decorum and epistolary convention through its "fireside vulgarity." It is a poem that defines the male and female body as the sum of their genital and excremental parts. Its catalogue of attributes, its coterie allusions, even its specificity of dating, make it the vulgar antitype to the Hawesean compilation of poem 13. This is not a poem of the *court Inperiall* but verses of the jakes, a poem that appeals not to the erotics of the courtly gaze but to the voyeurisms of the surreptitious viewer. It is, in essence, an anti-blazon— a poem written from the woman's view, one that dismembers human forms not into items of erotic delectation but, instead, into the objects of a voyeur's gaze. For the key point, it seems to me, that irrespective of its historical composition, its survival in this manuscript makes it a poem written down by a man's hand. Read in the context of its scribe's preoccupations with discovery and shame—and with his parallel predilections associating sexual and political transgression—this text becomes a textbook of voyeurism. It is, together with the Hawesean selections of the volume, testimony to what Freud saw as the importance of "visual impressions" in makings of "libidinal excitation." While Freud acknowledged the natural desire to behold, he considered such observance a perversion:

> (a) if it is restricted exclusively to the genitals, or (b) if it is connected with the overriding of disgust (as in the case of voyeurs or people who look at excretory functions) or (c) if, instead of being preparatory to the normal sexual aim, it supplants it. . . . The force which opposes scopophilia, but which may be overridden by it (in a manner parallel to what we have previously seen in the case of disgust) is shame.[40]

This is a poem, then, that makes its reader privy to the privy. Whatever the historicity of its composition, it is its transcription into Wellys's volume that renders it a spectacle of the transgressions of the female voice and body. It functions, I believe, in Wellys's book as something of an intercepted document: a letter found and transcribed by the very "Humffrey" who is there inscribed within it.

It also functions as but one more document of shame in the collections of a scribal voyeur. I have argued elsewhere that Wellys constructs himself as a "pandaric" reader—that he frames his project and arranges his material within a governing inspectory, illicit gaze, and that his manuscript presents a set of literary, if not psychoanalytic, problems about public shame and private delectation.[41] Though one might well resist the wholesale application of Freudian theory to this early sixteenth-century compiler, Freud's categories do explain, I think, something of Wellys's fascinations and, in turn, something of the compilatory tensions between poems such as numbers seven and thirteen in the collection. For what governs both is, I believe, that odd insertion of the Garter motto. It is here—as well as, say, in the surviving manuscript of *Sir Gawain and the Green Knight*—that we find the precise distillation of shame itself. The Garter motto, and the story of royal impropriety that stands behind it, is the locus of courtly shame and the place where we may fruitfully locate the anxieties surrounding the display of courtly bodies. Humphrey Wellys, much as perhaps the *Gawain*-poet (at least in Geraldine Heng's reading), seeks to negotiate that tension between scopophilia and shame: a tension between looking at the public body and imagining its private acts and parts.[42] The transcript of this scatological verse in Wellys's manuscript constitutes, perhaps, an act of voyeurism of a distinctively Freudian sort, much as the secretivity and surreption of this manuscript's assembly make Wellys himself into the early modern version of the peeping tom of Sartre and Barthes. This is, in short, a case not of the medieval writer as voyeur—as A. C. Spearing's recent book would have it—but a case of the *reader* as voyeur: and in particular, where what generates such a voyeurism is the early modern reading of medieval texts.

The Comforts of Reading

In reviewing the work of Stephen Hawes and what I have taken as his most subtle, yet powerfully intrusive early reader, Humphrey Wellys, I have been concerned with relations not just of the body and the book as images, or themes, or public practices, but as contributing to the idea of literary authorship and, as a consequence, of early modern subjectivity itself. The genre of the literary blazon dovetails, I wish to suggest, with the habit of the literary cento. Both locate the tension between reading books or bodies as integral wholes and fragmenting them into a set of readily available (or, perhaps, digestible) parts. What I am interested in, then, is the dismantling of major literary texts into new free-standing bodies. Wellys does this throughout his appropriation of Middle English literature: in his nine-stanza *Troilus* poem, in his chunk of Skelton's *Why Come Ye Nat to Courte*, in his Lydgatean lines, and in his Hawesean centos. Wellys's manuscript, I wish to claim, refigures the idea of the body of work. It makes the commonplace book into the body. The personal anthology becomes a blazon of a larger work: a selective dismembering that takes the individuated sections of a text and makes it the precious object of visual (or scribal) delectation. Reading is *blazonerie* for Wellys, and in this act of personal selection, the anthologist reenacts something of the visionary journey of the Hawesean hero. For through-out Hawes's allegories, his narrator/lovers always confront inscribed texts, engraved announcements, pictures offered up with cryptic or explanatory captions. The experience of loving for these heroes is inseparable from the life of reading, and I think what Humphrey Wellys learned from this literary life goes far beyond local appropriations or adaptings of a verbal legacy. Wellys learned a way of reading, a conception of the private and the public, a notion of literary subjectivity that depends directly on the confrontation of brief disembodied texts. As Hawes had put it in the *Conforte of Louers*, in those lines that define just what precisely "conforte" means,

> Two thynges me conforte/euer in pryncypall
> The fyrst be bokes/made in antyquyte
> By Gower and Chauncers/poetes rethorycall
> And Lydgate eke/by good auctoryte
> Makynge mencyon/of the felycyte
> Of my lady and me/by dame fortunes chaunce
> To me togyders / by wonderfull ordinaunce

> The seconde is / where fortune dooth me brynge
> In many placys / I se by prophecy
> As in the storyes / of the olde buyldynge

Letters for my lady / depeynted wonderly
And letters for me / besyde her meruayllously
Agreynge well / vnto my bokes all
In dyuers placys / I se it in generall.

(281–94)

So, too, did Humphrey Wellys find his "conforte." No longer
living in the realm of the "pastime," no longer focused on the
public eye, no longer viewing literature as the purview of the
courtly public or the public courtier, Wellys understands that true
"conforte" is to be found in books made by the canonical writers
of the Middle English tradition. He has sought in "dyuers placys"
his own "storyes" of love and loss, of surreption and discovery.
If, in the process, he has granted us a distinctively personal account of early English literature, he has also provided us with
something of a paradigm of early modern reading and, in turn,
with the outlines of the reception and the uses of medieval writing in the making of the courtly body.[43]

Notes

1. Seth Lerer, *Chaucer and His Readers: Imagining the Author in Late-Medieval
England* (Princeton: Princeton University Press, 1993), chaps. 5–6, pp.
147–208.

2. See my discussion in *Chaucer and His Readers*, 147–75, and for later
sixteenth-century editions, see Joseph A. Dane, "Who is Buried in
Chaucer's Tomb?—Prolegomena," *Huntington Library Quarterly* 57 (1994):
99–123.

3. See *Chaucer and His Readers*, 153–54, and Joseph B. Trapp, "Ovid's
Tomb," *Journal of the Warburg and Courtauld Institutes* 34 (1973): 33–76.

4. *Pastime of Pleasure*, 1336–37. See *Chaucer and His Readers*, 274 n.7. Detailed information may be found in A. S. G. Edwards, "Poet and Printer
in Sixteenth Century England: Stephen Hawes and Wynkyn de Worde,"
Gutenberg Jahrbuch (1980): 82–88, and "From Manuscript to Print: Wyn-

kyn de Worde and the Printing of Contemporary Poetry," *Gutenberg Jahr-buch* (1991): 143–48. In this paper, all quotations from Hawes's *Pastime of Pleasure* are from the edition of W. E. Mead, Early English Text Society, o.s., 173 (London: Oxford University Press, 1928), and from his other poetry from the edition of Florence Gluck and Alice B. Morgan, *Stephen Hawes: The Minor Poems*, Early English Text Society, o.s., 271 (London: Oxford University Press, 1974); citations will be identified by poem and line number in my text.

5. C. S. Lewis, *English Literature in the Sixteenth Century, Excluding Drama* (Oxford: Clarendon Press, 1954); John Stevens, *Music and Poetry at the Early Tudor Court* (London: Methuen, 1961); Raymond Southall, *The Courtly Maker* (Oxford: Blackwell, 1964); H. A. Mason, *Humanism and Poetry in the Early Tudor Period* (London: Routledge and Kegan Paul, 1959).

6. Beginning with Stephen Greenblatt, *Renaissance Self-Fashioning* (Chicago: University of Chicago Press, 1980), and continuing through Jonathan Crewe, *Trials of Authorship* (Berkeley and Los Angeles: University of California Press, 1990), and Jonathan Goldberg, *Sodometries* (Stanford: Stanford University Press, 1993).

7. *Renaissance Self-Fashioning*, 131.

8. David Carlson, "Reputation and Duplicity: The Texts and Contexts of Thomas More's Epigram on Bernard André," *ELH* 58 (1991): 261–81, the arguments of which have been incorporated in his *English Humanist Books* (Toronto: University of Toronto Press, 1993).

9. I, of course, appropriate this phrasing from Francis Barker, *The Tremulous Private Body* (London: Methuen, 1984).

10. André had been appointed historiographer and "poeta laureatus" to Henry VII by 1490; Skelton received the laureation from English and European universities and, by the ascension of Henry VIII, consistently thought of himself as poet laureate (see *Chaucer and His Readers*, 272 n. 46 and the bibliography cited therein). A. C. Spearing notices this allusion too (*From Medieval to Renaissance in English Poetry* [Cambridge: Cambridge University Press, 1985], 255).

11. For the details of Hawes's biography, together with interpretations of the information offered in de Worde's title pages and colophons, see A. S. G. Edwards, *Stephen Hawes* (Boston: Twayne, 1985). Edwards offers his own reading of the *Conforte* at pp. 77-87.

12. See "Representation Through Intimacy" in *Symbols and Sentiments*, ed. Ioan Lewis (London: Academic Press, 1977), 187–224 at 198. Star-

key's views have been put forward in a range of other publications, many of whose arguments and evidence overlap. See, in particular, "Intimacy and Innovation: The Rise of the Privy Chamber, 1485–1547" in *The English Court: From the Wars of the Roses to the Civil War*, ed. David Starkey (London: Longman, 1987), 71–118.

13. Alistair Fox, *Politics and Literature in the Reigns of Henry VII and Henry VIII* (Oxford: Blackwell, 1989), 56–72.

14. *Sodometries*, 29–61 at 39.

15. *Sodometries*, 54.

16. Hawes's advisory lady begins by counselling him, "Dyspayre you not / for it auayleth nought" (150), an echo of Pandarus's inaugural strategy at *Troilus and Criseyde* I.779–80: "Quod Pandarus, 'allas, what may this be, / That thow dispeired art thus causeles?'" Her remarks in the following line, "Ioye cometh after / whan the payne is gone" (151), are noted by Gluck and Morgan as echoing *Troilus* I.953, "And also ioie is next the fyn of sorwe." The maxim in the *Conforte*, "Clymbe not to fast / lest sodenly ye slyde" (157), resonates, too, with Pandarus's Boethian advice to get off Fortune's wheel. It is also worth noting that this line comes to stand as something of a maxim of courtier service in later satiric verse. In the *Testament of Papyngo* (c. 1530) by the Scots poet David Lyndsay, the court is full of "Pandaris, pykthankis, custronis, and clatteraris" (390). In discussing the "vaine ascens of court" (351), he notes, "Quho sittith moist hie sal fynd the sait most slider" (352). These quotations are from *The Works of Sir David Lindsay of the Mount*, ed. Douglas Hamer, vol. 1 (Edinburgh: Scottish Text Society, 1931).

17. See, for example, the discussion of these aspects of the poem in R. A. Shoaf, *Dante, Chaucer, and the Currency of the Word* (Norman: Pilgrim Books, 1983), 115–22, and Chauncey Wood, *The Elements of Chaucer's Troilus* (Durham: Duke University Press, 1984), 143–64.

18. See, for example the accounts of the poem in Carolyn Dinshaw, *Chaucer's Sexual Poetics* (Madison: University of Wisconsin Press, 1989), esp. 82; Elaine Tuttle Hansen, *Chaucer and the Fictions of Gender* (Berkeley: University of California Press, 1993), esp. 50ff.

19. *Renaissance Self-Fashioning*, 124–25.

20. For Carroz, see his letter to Ferdinand of Spain, 29 May 1510, in *Supplement to Volume I and Volume II of Letters, Dispatches, and State Papers Relating to the Negotiations Between England and Spain*, ed. G. A. Bergenroth (London: Public Record Office, 1868), 36–44.

21. Desiderius Erasmus, *De conscribendis epistolis*, trans. Charles Fantazzi, in *CollectedWorks of Erasmus* (Toronto: University of Toronto Press, 1985), 25:195. For the Latin text see *De conscribendis epistolis*, ed. Jean-Claude Margolin, in *Opera omnia Desiderii Erasmi Roterodami* (Amsterdam: North Holland, 1971), 1.2:499–500.

22. See Lawrence D. Kritzman, *The Rhetoric of Sexuality and the Literature of the French Renaissance* (Cambridge: Cambridge University Press, 1991), 97–111.

23. Nancy J. Vickers, "Diana Described: Scattered Woman and Scattered Rhyme," *Critical Inquiry* 8 (1981): 265–79; Kritzman, *Rhetoric of Sexuality*, esp. 97–111.

24. Edwards briefly discusses Hawes's references to the word "pastime" in the poem, though without their apposition to "conforte" (*Stephen Hawes*, 82–83).

25. For a detailed analysis of these texts, together with an edition of the entire manuscript, see *The Welles Anthology, MS. Rawlinson C. 813*, ed. Sharon L. Jansen and Kathleen H. Jordan (Binghamton: Medieval and Renaissance Texts and Studies, 1991). Unless otherwise specified, all quotations from the Rawlinson text will be from this edition, cited by item number and line number in my text. Jansen and Jordan's work has come under serious critique by Edward Wilson. For his work on Wellys (whose spelling of the family name I follow), see "Local Habitations and Names in MS. Rawlinson C. 813 in the Bodleian Library," *Review of English Studies*, n. s., 41 (1990): 12–44, and "The Testament of the Buck and the Sociology of the Text," *Review of English Studies*, n. s., 45 (1994): 157–84. My arguments about Wellys's work here develop some suggestions (and occasionally appropriate some of the phrasings) at the close of *Chaucer and His Readers*, 213–18.

26. For some examples, see *Chaucer and His Readers*, 215–16.

27. Jansen and Jordan, *The Welles Anthology*, 124.

28. See Walter Ullman, "This Realm of England is an Empire," *Journal of Ecclesiastical History* 30 (1979): 175–204; John Guy, "Thomas Cromwell and the Intellectual Origins of the Henrician Revolution," in *Reassessing the Henrician Age*, ed. Alistair Fox and John Guy (Oxford: Blackwell, 1986).

29. Wilson, "Local Habitations," 12–17.

30. G. R. Elton, *Policy and Police* (Cambridge: Cambridge University Press, 1972), 383.

31. I am summarizing here a great deal of material concerning the status of the king's signature and sign during the 1530s, together with public and political anxieties about seditious writing and encrypting. For the basic laws, see Statutes of the Realm, 27 Hen.VIII.2 and 31 Hen.VIII.14. For some broader approaches to these anxieties, see Starkey, "Court and Government," in *Revolution Reassessed*, ed. Christopher Coleman and David Starkey (Oxford: Oxford University Press, 1986), 46–55.

32. Wilson, "Local Habitations," 30.

33. See the discussion and analysis of the Devonshire Manuscript (London, British Library, Add. 17492) in Paul G. Remley, "Mary Shelton and her Tudor Literary Milieu," in *Rethinking the Henrician Era: Essays on Early Tudor Texts and Contexts*, ed. Peter C. Herman (Urbana: University of Illinois Press, 1994), 40–77. Several of the poems in this manuscript are made up of stanzas drawn from *Troilus and Criseyde* (as well as from other poems printed in Thynne's Chaucer edition of 1532), and Remley argues that such adaptations articulate not only the illicit relationship between Margaret Douglas and Thomas Howard (51), but also give voice to Mary Shelton's "indignation at the treatment of women of her time by hypocritical lovers" (56).

34. Jansen and Jordan, *The Welles Anthology*, 124.

35. Wilson, "Local Habitations," 15. For the text of this inscription, see Jansen and Jordan, *The Welles Anthology*, 1–3, and for a somewhat different reading and interpretation see Wilson, 14–15.

36. For a recent review of the gendered epistolics of the *Troilus*, see Sarah Stanbury, "Women's Letters and Private Space in Chaucer," *Exemplaria* 6 (1994): 271–84.

37. My text is from Wilson, "Local Habitations," who offers a better transcription of the manuscript than Jansen and Jordan do. I have, however, presented here some emendations of my own (mostly of capitalization and punctuation). I also gloss some of the more obscure phrasings in the margin.

38. Wilson, "Local Habitations," 24–25.

39. Wilson, "Local Habitations," 44.

40. *Three Essays in the Theory of Sexuality*, in *The Standard Edition of the Complete Psychological Works of Sigmund Freud* (London: Hogarth, 1953–74), 7:149–50. This text, and its larger critical reception, form the core of several recent attempts to understand the nature of male vision and

female beholding in late medieval literature. In particular, it is the theoretical springboard for A. C. Spearing, *The Medieval Poet as Voyeur* (Cambridge: Cambridge University Press, 1993), and to a certain degree for
Sarah Stanbury, especially her essay "The Voyeur and the Private Life in
Troilus and Criseyde," *Studies in the Age of Chaucer* 13 (1991): 141–58. Let me
take this opportunity here, however, to clarify my terminology. I am in
no way approving of Freud's definitions of "perversion" here. Indeed,
Freud himself seemed anxious about such a designation: "No healthy
person, it appears, can fail to make some addition that might be called
perverse to the normal sexual aim; and the universality of this finding is
in itself enough to show how inappropriate it is to use the word perversion as a term of reproach" ("The Perversions in General," *Standard
Edition* 7:161). Much more work needs to be done in explicating the
Freudian paradigms of voyeurism and scopophilia, especially in relationship to earlier historical texts and social practices.

41. *Chaucer and His Readers,* 213–18.

42. Geraldine Heng, "A Woman Wants: The Lady, *Gawain,* and the
Forms of Seduction," *Yale Journal of Criticism* 5 (1992): 101–34.

43. This essay draws on material from my forthcoming book, *Courtly
Letters in the Age of Henry VIII* (Cambridge: Cambridge University Press
1997).

CHAPTER FOUR

Getting Medieval: *Pulp Fiction,* Gawain, Foucault

Carolyn Dinshaw

Quentin Tarantino's Middle Ages

My title derives from some lines in a dark scene deep within *Pulp Fiction.* They are spoken by Ving Rhames as Marsellus Wallace, the big black boss presiding over the underworld of the movie—that world's heretofore unmoved mover. To this point all we have seen of him is the back of the neck. Due to circumstances definitely beyond his control, Marsellus has been raped by a sadistic white southerner in an S/M dungeon; and after he has been rescued by the very man he has been pursuing, Butch Coolidge (Bruce Willis), he snarls back to "Mr. Rapist," now shot in the crotch and writhing on the floor:

> I'm gonna call a coupla pipe-hittin' niggers, who'll go to work on homes here with a pair of pliers and a blow torch.
> (to Zed)
> Hear me talkin' hillbilly boy?! I ain't through with you by a damn sight. I'm gonna git Medieval on your ass.[1]

Get Medieval. The phrase caught on like wildfire: street-smart teenage boys (the "young male viewers" whom *Variety* pegged as an obvious primary audience for this movie) could be heard in San Francisco slinging the phrase around the neighborhood; Courtney Love, speaking of her dead husband, Kurt Cobain (reluctant idol of such teenage boys), picked it up to describe how she wanted to treat his remains;[2] magazine headlines used it; *Saturday Night Live* created a skit around it; *Film Threat* magazine in early 1995 voted Ving Rhames "Bastard of the Year" for pronouncing the phrase, and noted approvingly, "Ving gets bonus points for combining the words *ass* and *medieval* in the same sentence."[3] The phrase has entered American public culture. Why has it proved so popular? What exactly makes it so useful? To get a clue, I want to look first at what it means in this film: why this word here? What function does it perform other than to inflict a slight sting on the medievalist, buried in the past but finally getting out to see a movie?

The phrase isn't repeated in the fast-talking film; the Middle Ages aren't mentioned again. But we medievalists, instead of sinking even lower beneath the pop-culture surface, might instead conceive of ourselves as specially equipped to view this movie. With a whole armature of narratives and images that look in fact very much like *Pulp Fiction*, medievalists can suggest ways in which what is seen to be Hollywood's latest—from the hot-hot-hot Quentin Tarantino—is indeed a very old story. But that isn't a point simply to gloat over; rather, keeping in mind the past's difference even as we chart its continuities in the present, we can suggest that the future offers possibilities of still other, profoundly different, narratives and lives. In this essay I want to play *Pulp Fiction*'s use of the medieval alongside my use of a fourteenth-century text (whose cultural agenda, I argue, *Pulp Fiction* has inherited), and then to bring to bear on these two modern-day uses another one—Foucault's—whose thematic preoccupations unite it to these, while its political intentions mark its radicality.

Back, then, to the dungeon. There's a lot of violence in *Pulp Fiction*, lots of gore splattered: on my count, five bodies blown away altogether onscreen, an additional three wounded, plus two others busted offscreen or in the prehistory of the narrative—not counting the casualties in this scene. Violence happens routinely; it causes practical problems ("Now you got a corpse in a car, minus a head, in a garage. Take me to it," says Harvey Keitel as Mr. Wolf, who fixes messes [128]). One hit man's qualms (in the film's last scene) cannot alter the whole moral economy: killing, maiming, and terrorizing are what happens, and they continue to happen in the in-folded narrative events that diegetically occur *after* the film's last scene.

But in the dark scene with which I began, in the dungeon-basement of the "Mason-Dixon Pawnshop," with its sadomasochism and its southern proprietors, there is what *Time* magazine, picking up on the film's priorities, called "a fate worse than death": not only rape, but, crucially, sodomitical rape.[4] Butch, having freed himself from the sadists' bonds and fleeing the perverts' pawnshop, suddenly hesitates; he decides he can't leave Marsellus, his mortal enemy, "in a situation like that" (scr 105), and selects the largest weapon the pawnshop has to offer in order to free his enemy from being sodomized: not the hammer, not the chainsaw, not the Louisville slugger, but a "magnificent" Samurai sword (scr 106). After Butch stealthily returns to the basement and "THRUSTS" it into one of the brothers (scr 107), Marsellus is freed from the other startled brother, shoots him in the crotch, and makes his medieval plans: as was the provision of a secular law in France in 1270 (whose terms are not unique by any means in the Western Middle Ages), the punishment for sodomy was castration for the first offense, death by fire for repeat offenders—kind of like pliers and a blow torch.[5]

The sodomitical violence in this scene is different from any other violence in the film, and it calls for a different remedy: it is ritualized sexual torture, it is dark and perverse, and it must be met by a personal vengeance that is itself ritualized, torturous, dark, and perverse. This is the realm of the medieval in *Pulp Fiction*:

it isn't exactly another *time*, in this movie in which time is peculiarly flattened out both by the manipulations of narrative and by the drenching of everything in postwar cinematic and pop culture references; Marsellus's line about "a pair of pliers and a blow torch" is in fact a direct quotation from the 1973 cult gangster movie *Charley Varrick*.[6] The medieval, rather, is the space of the rejects—really, the abjects—of this world. Despite the *New York Times*'s liberal claim that the film is "completely and amicably integrated," we can see what must be eliminated: sodomy, sadomasochism, southerners.[7] Even the status of black men is degraded by this scene, despite the fact that it is a black man who speaks these lines and who clearly participates in the process of abjecting those country perverts. At the end of this sequence we're left with the vision of the triumphant Butch, roaring away on the Harley owned by the homo whose medieval torture is being planned—white hypermasculine Butch, drawing on the sexually powerful look of a macho gay man but whose ass, we know for sure now, is straight, male, modern.

We might well have wondered about Butch's butthole. The film plants the doubt itself. In a scene at least one critic found gratuitous,[8] the dream that chronologically begins his story, Butch recalls that as a young boy he was visited by a Vietnam War buddy of his father's. Captain Koons, played by Christopher Walken, tells the young Butch the story of the gold watch that he is now delivering from Butch's dead father, who didn't make it out of "that Hanoi pit of hell" (67). I'm always interested in what seems gratuitous in a narrative, since these are the things that, for some reason, the author simply can't leave out. What we get here is not just a "gross-out . . . anecdote" (Janet Maslin) or a lousy "joke" (Anthony Lane); the anatomy, as it were, of male bonding—the relationship of homosocial and homosexual male relations in this movie about gangsters—is opened to view.

In a deadpan monologue, Captain Koons tells the little Butch that the watch he is being given was his "great granddaddy's war watch" from the First World War, handed down to his "granddad for good luck" in World War II, in turn handed down to his infant father, who grew up to be "shot down over Hanoi" with the watch on his wrist:

> Now he knew if the gooks ever saw the watch it'd be confiscated. The way your Daddy looked at it, that watch was your birthright. And he'd be damned if any slopeheads were gonna put their greasy yella hands on his boy's birthright. So he hid it in the one place he knew he could hide somethin'. His ass. Five long years, he wore this watch up his ass. Then when he died of dysentery, he gave me the watch. I hid this uncomfortable hunk of metal up my ass for two years. Then, after seven years, I was sent home to my family. And now, little man, I give the watch to you. (68)

The Captain puts a "hunk" up his ass, the same "hunk" that has been up his buddy's ass; the suggestions of sodomy are obvious. They're only suggestions, of course: the hunk is "uncomfortable," not pleasurable; there's no necessary anal contact between the giver and the receiver of the watch; and the detail about death from dysentery works hard to make the whole monologue laughably disgusting. Sodomy is only hinted at here, both suggested and at the same time deflected into a sophomoric shit joke.[9]

But what is clearly confirmed in this initial scene is the centrality of the anus in male bonding, or, more precisely, in the maintenance of patriarchy: the inter-anal transportation and handing-down of the watch from father to son ("little man") is the monologue's focus. What is not clear is the limit of the uses of the anus between and among men. This is an issue obsessively raised in Tarantino's films (including the *True Romance* screenplay, *Reservoir Dogs*, and even his bit part in *Sleep With Me*) but never patiently worked out. In ways more superficial and conservative than in the deeper and more pointed—yet still unresolved—*Reservoir Dogs*, the whole Butch episode undertakes to limit the uses of the anus.[10] We might call this episode's project "anus-surveillance," following John J. Winkler's studies of classical Athens: sodomy, implicitly suggested and denied in the opening monologue as a possibility in male bonding, is then explicitly represented, in the pawnshop basement, as unconsensual and violent—rape—so that it can't be seen as in any way acceptable.[11] In this racist straight white male imaginary, sodomy is, as well, represented as most demeaning: it puts you in the passive and feminine, which is equal to the black, position here. Sodomy is combined with sadomasochism, which figures sexual torture as an unmistakable perversion and thus safely distances the everyday torture hit men perform from any perverse desire.[12] Butch can ride off on that chopper with his French girlfriend (who insists that he give her "oral pleasure" before she does him [81]); he can even "hum[p] a hot hog," as the script puts it (109, probably referring particularly to *Deliverance*); he can look like a Castro fag; and because of these representational strategies the audience can still rest assured that his straight masculinity is unthreatened. Earlier in the movie, the marriage of queer "love birds"—the Three Stooges—is broadcast on a TV Lance the drug dealer is watching ("Hold hands, you love birds," we hear); but that queer parody is comfortingly replaced by the real thing now: as the final stage directions for this episode read, "the two lovebirds [Butch and Fabian (sic)] PEEL AWAY" (scr 111) on the chopper.

This anal surveillance project makes sense, too, of the fact that John Travolta, as Vincent Vega, spends so much time on the toilet in this movie. He misses out on crucial action twice when he goes, as he puts it, to "take a shit" (and once when he "take[s] a piss"). This is part of the film's anal project: it is trying to reassure the putatively straight audience by this reminder that anuses *are* used for shitting. But that fact might not turn out to be so reassuring, after all.[13] Vince's time in the toilet has been not only useful but pleasurable—he dallies in a leisurely read of an action novel at Butch's apartment—and thus its distinction from another pleasurable use of the anus becomes blurred. Shitting is problematic in this movie, as Sharon Willis has shown; just as little Butch's father is said to have died of it, Vince himself must be eliminated. He's blown apart by Butch, the film's representation of the triumph of homo/hetero distinction.

Homosexual sex is a constant possibility between men, Tarantino's movies affirm. In major and minor moments throughout Pulp Fiction, the possibility of homosex is raised in an attempt to manage it—to distance and foreclose it. The attempt to construct straight white maleness and armor its body is thorough: men's bodies, black and white, must remain on guard against the possibilities of pleasurable opening. But by the end of the film, one black man has been "fuck[ed] . . . like a bitch" (as Jules puts it, referring to another situation [24]); the "armour" of Vince's and Jules's black suits, as Tarantino said in an interview, has been completely stripped off and turned into "the exact antithesis," volleyball wear;[14] and Vince is a lost cause in the project of constructing masculinity. As it turns out, neither Vince nor Jules can finally survive in this world in which any play with open and shut, clear-cut, and stable sexual distinctions proceeds according to an all-too-predictable straight white male agenda.

The medieval signals all the abjected Others of this world of Pulp Fiction. But as with all such abjection, the medieval lies at the heart of the modern, perversion lies at the heart of the straight, hicks at the heart of the urban, black at the heart of white. The very postmodern Pulp Fiction's concern to police the borders of male homosociality is continuous with medieval attempts at drawing the line (as we'll see below). Marsellus's "pipe-hittin'" city "niggers" will end up acting like the white hillbilly sadist they're torturing; similarly, Butch "THRUSTS" (scr 107) his giant, uh, sword into the other homo. And shortly after he has rescued Marsellus, Butch's question sounds like a proposition: "what now, between me and you?" (108). If the medieval represents things that can't be eradicated, despite efforts to construct something free of them—represents, that is, the impurity of these apparently pure concepts (straightness, whiteness, identity), then "getting medieval" redoubles that impurity by making the medieval (the abject) itself a role or game. Getting medieval—playing in an abjected space, adopting an abjected role—doubly gets at the impossibility of absolute straightness, whiteness, modernity, of the purely dominant, of essentially being anything. And this condition of inessentiality, the basic condition of the impossibility of essential identity, becomes an explicit problem at the film's end. It is an impossibility so thorough in this postmodern cinematic world of simulation and citation that it takes a putative miracle from God to suggest—to Jules, the hit man with qualms—any chance of being (as he puts it) "just . . . Jules . . . no more, no less" (147). Being, not just acting.

Jules worries, at last, about his own rituals of performance as he struggles to extract himself from a world in which he and Vince "get into character" (17) in order to stage a killing: he's been accustomed to quote a Biblical text just before he blows his victims away, but what role is it, exactly, he wonders, that he's been playing in the Ezekiel verses he quotes? (157–58). That he could worry about the potential interchangeability of roles in themselves means that he must already be through with this acting and this whole world. As the character—black—in whom authenticity has been located in the film, he prefers, as he states at the end, to wander the earth "Until God puts me where he wants me to be" (147, emphasis added). Jules is the only one trying to opt out at this point, and the figure of Jimmie (formerly in the life and still plagued by his hit-man pal) suggests that any break Jules tries to make isn't going to be clean. Furthermore, in the racist "new world order" of this film, as bell hooks notes, the "resident black male preacher/philosopher death-dealing mammified intellectual," thus enlightened, doesn't have anywhere to go: Vince makes it clear that Jules will be a bum if he quits.[15]

Jules's isn't the only response to the impossibility of true identity, of course, to simulation and roles, in this movie whose deepest (and most expensive) visual delight is the simulation of a simulated '50s diner in '90s L.A. The film revels in role-playing so deeply that its own actors refer to their earlier roles: John Travolta's dancing the twist and Christopher Walken's POW monologue are the most obvious examples. But it's crucial to remember that shaping all this revelling is the film's desire to limit what, exactly, can be performed and by whom—which roles or positions can be taken up as empowering and which ones can't. This is an agenda that has used Jules, as various critics point out, to articulate its own desire for authenticity, for the solid ground of being. Dennis Cooper has remarked on Tarantino's "fascination with the amoral," a fascination that is itself "moralistic."[16]

But couldn't *Pulp Fiction*, then, for all the obviousness of its asshole narrative, for all its joy in cross-race male homosociality, be pointing out and critiquing homophobia? Couldn't it be critiquing the way homophobia dissolves even racial boundaries in its corrosive patriarchal politics? Butch can't leave the black man "in a situation like that"; sodomy is the worst thing, bar no explosive violence, in the world of this movie. Isn't Tarantino showing how absurd an attitude this is? Maybe, at times; there's certainly a send-up of *Deliverance* in this scene. But with bell hooks, who has posed these questions as well, I contend that it doesn't finally *matter* if you read it that way or not, if you catch the parody or if you don't:

> Yeah, like it's really funny when Butch the hypermasculine phallic white boy—who has no name that means anything, who has no culture to be proud of, who comes straight out of childhood clinging to the anal-retentive timepiece of patriarchal imperialism—is exposed. Yet exposure does nothing to intervene on this evil, it merely graphically highlights it.[17]

Jules, she points out further, is not shown grieving or seeking revenge for Vince when he's blown away: so much for enduring
male bonding. And if it's a twist on the usual scenario that this
black man isn't killed, no place to which he tries to exit will have
changed: as Sharon Willis remarks more mildly, "we need to en-
tertain the possibility that *Pulp Fiction* might resecure racialized
representations for a racist imaginary, even as it tries to work
them loose from it." [18]

Subversive possibility may "titillate" in a narrative sequence
such as "The Gold Watch," but then "everything," as hooks observes, "kinda comes right back to normal." [19] Band-Aids will still
be made in the color "flesh," like the one that sticks, gleaming, to
Marsellus's black neck; and the black woman will still be a just-
barely-visible phantasm. [20] White Butch and Fabian have places to
go (Bora Bora, Tahiti, Mexico? [83]) and a big bike, courtesy of
a dead homosexual, to take them there. And Jules, not mourn-
ing for Vince, will wander without arriving anywhere and will
continue to represent authenticity for a sped-up dominant culture—the culture in and of this film, including the hordes of
its appreciative viewers—that revels in but ultimately fears really
getting medieval.

My Middle Ages

It may seem that at this point I'm going to produce a *real* medieval text with which to beat Tarantino's pop culture fiction of
the Middle Ages to a pulp. But of course I have my agenda, too;
I'm not only a medievalist but a *queer* medievalist in the cinematic audience. My Middle Ages, informed as it is by primary
and secondary materials, is nonetheless as political as is his. I'm
with Umberto Eco, who itemizes "Ten Little Middle Ages," and
challenges us to accept

> the moral and cultural duty of spelling out what kind of Middle
> Ages we are talking about. To say openly which of the above ten

types we are referring to means to say who we are and what we dream of, if we are simply practicing a more or less honest form of divertissement, if we are wondering about our basic problems or if we are supporting, perhaps without realizing it, some new reactionary plot.[21]

Tarantino draws on an idea of the medieval momentarily and casually, without concern for historicity, in a "divertissement" that nonetheless reveals a complex ideology—an idea of the medieval that ends up supporting (as I've just argued) a "reactionary plot." In my use of the medieval I both openly engage an idea of the Middle Ages and make a certain claim about its historical existence. With Eco, I view the Middle Ages as a time when basic structures, and basic problems, of modern Western culture were in the making, including

> modern languages, merchant cities, capitalist economy. . . . The rise of modern armies, of the modern concept of the national state . . . ; the struggle between the poor and the rich, the concept of heresy or ideological deviation, even our contemporary notion of love as a devastating unhappy happiness. I could add the conflict between church and state, trade unions . . . the technological transformation of labor. . . . The Middle Ages are the root of all our contemporary "hot" problems.[22]

Though Eco doesn't mention sex or sexuality in his ten Middle Ages, he does mention the medieval origins of contemporary love. And I want to extend that point; the construction of straight white masculinity I have discussed in *Pulp Fiction* has a long history that I, as a queer medievalist, have a particular interest in tracing. In my assertion of a relation between then and now, between *Sir Gawain and the Green Knight* and *Pulp Fiction*, lies my political investment in the Western Middle Ages.

To begin to dig up those long roots, then, I want to turn to a genre that has a lot in common with the gangster crime genre for which Tarantino has become famous: the Arthurian chivalric romance. After all, what's more Arthurian than *Pulp Fiction*'s gangsters, dressed in their black suits of "armour," performing tasks for a central lord, bonding as brothers, going off on adventures, splattering blood and gore, facing death? What's more Arthurian than a watch-amulet, symbol of fierce filial loyalty? Than a mistress from a far-off land? Than riding off on a superbly looked-after animal, a "hog"? Than names that are full of descriptive significance? What's more Arthurian than being seduced by the lord's wife while he is away? Than a solitary debate of issues of loyalty to one's lord? Than having a character central to the narrative with a nick on his neck?

If that last is pure coincidence with *Sir Gawain and the Green Knight*, as I am certain it is, the other thematic similarities I've just enumerated are far from happenstance: they're part and parcel of romance plotting, the conventions of which are familiar to anyone steeped in American or European pop culture. And the romance narrative genre has a big ostensible task: to promote heterosexuality against all odds.[23] What's more chivalric than homosexual relations, often troubling the borders of knightly terrain? We find explicit accusations in earlier French romance, a tradition to which SGGK is indebted—in *Lanval*, in the *Eneas*, as well.[24] The Galehaut episode in the Prose *Lancelot* suggests that male-male *fine amor* might be as intense a motive for adventures as the male-female variety.[25] Further, just as *Pulp Fiction*'s sexual politics intersects with its race politics, so, in a related way, does a proto-nationalist agenda frame SGGK's romance of the Christian knight: the fall of Troy brackets the narrative of SGGK, a poem with ties to the court of Richard II in London (the "new Troy"), suggesting that a threat to straight Christian chivalric identity is at the same time a threat to national identity, to Englishness.[26] I want to uncover the homosexual potential between knights in SGGK, to see how such anus-surveillance as I observed in *Pulp Fiction* is at work earlier here, and to see how it is linked, as it is in the movie, with the problem of essential identity. I want to suggest that the queer medievalist's use of the poem can resist its straightening force. The inessentiality associated with the medieval in *Pulp Fiction*, on the one hand, and the crisis of identity in the medieval *SGGK*, on the other, both represented as finally unbearable, in other contexts can be valued differently—and Foucault, in his vision of the medieval, takes them as opportunities for liberation.

But now to the plot of *SGGK*.[27] Here's the situation in Fitt Three of the poem: Gawain, a guest in Bertilak's castle, Hautdesert, has agreed to play an exchange of winnings game with his host—to give Bertilak everything he receives in the course of his pursuits during the day; Bertilak will in turn give Gawain everything he gets. This agreement is renewed twice, so that exchanges between the two men occur three times, three days running. Bertilak spends each day on a hunt (for a doe on the first day, a boar on the second, and finally a fox). Gawain, back in the castle, is involved in a sort of indoor hunt: the Lady creeps into his bedroom and tries to seduce him into sleeping with her while her husband is off in the woods. She gets as far as to persuade him to accept a kiss from her on the first day, two kisses on the second, and three kisses and a love token on the third.

Each evening the two exchange the spoils of the day. Bertilak proudly presents his winnings to Gawain, triumphantly rehearsing tales of his hunting adventures. Gawain, in turn, renders each kiss he has received, and the narrative description of his manner here echoes his manner in the bedroom. The kisses were seductive, erotic in their first instance; are they now? Invoking the precise letter of their bargain, Gawain refuses to answer Bertilak's questions about them.

To complicate the consideration of those kisses: keep in mind that if Gawain had succumbed fully to the lady's seduction, *and* if he had honored the terms of his promise to the lord, he would in fact have had to have sex with the lord—to give over his winnings, that is, his sexual conquest, in his own body, just as he has done with the kisses he received. Male homosexual sex is thus one hypothetical fulfillment, a logical end of the interlocking plots the Lady and Bertilak enact—but it is a forbidden end. Or rather, not forbidden, but rendered impossible and insignificant within the explicitly hetero culture of this poem. Male homosexual relations are in this way fully *inside* the culture of the poem (produced by the games the three are playing) however apparently *outside* it (finally incomprehensible: Gawain and Bertilak?). Just as *Pulp Fiction* (in its more explicit manner) hints at sodomitical relations between war buddies only in order to distance actual sodomy and cleanse buddy/gangster relations of any taint, so *SGGK*, in its project to perpetuate heterosexuality, both produces the possibility of male homosexual relations between knights (signalled by those kisses) *and* renders them insignificant: those kisses can and must *mean nothing*—or, truer and worse, any threat they might pose is neutralized.

It's certainly true that innocent kisses often occur between men at moments of heightened emotion in late Middle English texts—just kisses, as when Arthur and his court regretfully kiss Gawain goodbye as he sets out on his journey (596). Such kisses represent conventional cultural practice, informed by the rules of courtesy and hospitality; there is nothing problematic about men's kissing one another *per se* in the medieval romance context, as there might be today in the United States. The poem's audience is surely used to seeing representations of kisses of peace, of greeting, of partings, of homage, and so on, between men.[28] Yet the narrative of *SGGK* locates the particular kisses between Bertilak and Gawain in reference to a highly-charged erotic plot and thus raises the question of their sexual force and valence. Further, as I detail later, erotic bonds between knights, as Jonathan Goldberg and Alan Bray have argued, might have gone unrecognized as sodomy, as long as they did not disturb heterosexual marriage arrangements and inheritance patterns; yet the poem—in this regard unlike the prose *Lancelot*—distinctly sets these kisses in relation to heterosexual adultery and thus, I contend, tips the chivalric homosocial balance toward homosexual—sodomitical—relations. As with other disturbing Middle English kisses, such as the Pardoner's and the Host's in the *Canterbury Tales*, we are thus on complex and difficult terrain, with the kisses in Fitt Three circulating erotic power. How has the poem neutralized that power? And what can we, readers with a queer agenda, make of those kisses, given to Bertilak by Gawain acting like a woman?

Gawain acts like a woman. The *acting like* is crucial here. *SGGK* is a poem heavily laden with the burden of identity: Gawain's symbol on his shield, for example, is the pentangle. With its interlocking lines and perfectly congruent angles delineating the "endeles" (630) unity of Gawain's physical, moral, and spiritual person, the pentangle is the poem's major and most insistent attempt to represent a unified identity, inside and out: "Forþy hit acordez to þis kny3t and to his cler armez" ("Therefore it accords with this knight and his bright arms" [631]).[29] This is a unity of properly masculine chivalric acts, properly directed desire (both earthly and spiritual), and proper body (the "wyttez," the "fyngres" [i.e., strength]). Yet that unified essence, that identity, is threatened in the bedroom scenes of seduction, in which the Lady appropriates the knight's position as active courtly lover; and that feminization, as I'll suggest, repeated in Gawain's acting like the woman who kissed him, precipitates a textual vision of violent dismemberment.

In the bedroom Gawain is the hunted, the object of a woman's gaze. The lady slips into his bedchamber in the morning while he sleeps, "ful dernly and stylle" ("very secretly and softly" [1188]) draws the door to behind her, and waits for him to stir:

> And ho stepped stilly and stel to his bedde,
> Kest vp þe cortyn and creped withinne,

And set hir ful softly on þe bed-syde,
And lenged þere selly longe to loke quen he wakened.
                                        (1191–94)

[And she stepped stealthily and stole to his bed, cast up
the curtain and crept inside, and sat herself very gently on
the bedside, and lingered there wondrously long to see his
waking.]

Her long look fixes him, or at least intends to do so, just as, earlier, the poem has made him the object of her gaze on his first
night at the castle: as Sheila Fisher has observed, when he is led
in to Vespers by her husband, she peers out of her pew at this
new arrival: "Into a cumly closet coyntly ho entrez. . . . / þenne
lyst þe lady to loke on þe kny3t" ("She goes into a comely
closed pew. . . . / Then the lady desired to look at the knight"
[934, 941]).[30] Now, keeping him unclothed and horizontal in
his bed, she has him "prysoun," prisoner, as he puts it (1219).
She has greeted him by name—"God moroun, Sir Gawayn"
("Good morning, Sir Gawain" [1208])—and a few lines later,
she reiterates that name and specifies its significance:

For I wene wel, iwysse, Sir Wowen 3e are,
þat alle þe worlde worchipez quere-so 3e ride;
Your honour, your hendelayk is hendely praysed.
                                        (1226–28)

[For well I know, indeed, that you're Sir Gawain,
whom all the world worships wherever you ride; your
honor, your courtesy is courteously praised.]

After nominally laying hold of him she introduces her intentions:

3e ar welcum to my cors,
Yowre awen won to wale,

Me behouez of fyne force
Your seruaunt be, and schale.
(1237–40)

[You are welcome to my person
<or: body>, to take your own
pleasure; <or: abode>; I must
of necessity be your servant,
and shall be.]

The reversal of courtly roles here couldn't be clearer, and it
seems the poet's conscious choice when we consider traditional
analogues (depicting either very active or passive wives here).[31]
Her gaze fixes him, she names him, she offers herself as his servant, whereas just the night before, greeting the lady and her
older companion for the first time, he offered himself as their
"seruaunt" (976).

It's no surprise, then, that the conversation is punctuated with
signs of identity confusion, mistakes, failure. When the lady first
slips into his bedchamber, Gawain pretends to sleep, and inter-
nally schemes to find out what she's up to. He may seem self-
possessed and wily then, and in the next moment cunningly
picks up her talk of truce and bondage by calling himself her
prisoner (1210–20); but he might seem rather less solid when
he doesn't recognize himself as the knight she is addressing, the
knight known to all: "I be not now he þat 3e of speken" ("I'm
not he of whom you speak" [1242; cf. 1243–44; 1266]). This is
courtly politesse, of course, and it goes on: he tries to counter
her construction of himself as her master when he offers himself as her servant (1278). And she flirtatiously interjects that
since he hasn't requested a kiss from her he can't be Gawain at
all: "Bot þat 3e be Gawan, hit gotz in mynde" ("It slips my mind
that you're Gawain" [1293]).

But courtly games—literal and figurative fencing—such as this one, with its role reversals, are in fact a serious business for Gawain, whose identity is understood to be so seamless a unity of internal nature and external act, of moral, physical, and spiritual: Gawain, responding to the lady's challenge to his identity *as* Gawain, indeed allows her a kiss, as if he is attempting to reconfirm his status *as* Gawain, the one who kisses (1302–6).[32] But on the following day the solidity of his identity is again denied because of what he hasn't done—claim a kiss: the bedroom conversation opens with a conditional that might sound downright threatening in this context: "Sir, 3if 3e be Wawen . . ." ("Sir, if you are Gawain . . ." [1481, emphasis added]). Time and time again through the course of the poem Gawain is told, when he is not acting like the reputed Gawain, that he is not, after all, Gawain (see also 2270). When his active role is usurped by the lady here, when he is not *doing*, he has no proper, courtly, masculine identity.[33]

The pentangle is never mentioned by name again in the narrative after its intricate introduction in Fitt Two,[34] and instead there is a vision of complete crisis when Gawain's seamless knightly identity is put at risk by the Lady's acts. Gawain's indoor seduction is linked to Bertilak's outdoor hunt by juxtaposition, as those two tightly interlaced sets of scenes are bound together with conjunctions (lines 1178–79, 1319, 1560–61, 1730–31, 1893–94). The feminizing role reversal inside the bedroom is mirrored on the first day by Bertilak's choice of prey: Gawain and female deer—barren hinds and does—are hunted in narrative tandem. The animal whose slaughter is described is the mirror image of Gawain: finally killed, her throat is cut, the limbs are cut off, the doe is eviscerated, and her insides are unlaced (cf. 1334). In a passage whose length has always been a puzzle—we know the gentry must have loved this detail, but it does seem excessive in this carefully structured romance, and such detail is repeated in the narration of the following two hunts (of male animals)—the animal body is split to pieces. I suggest that this unlacing of the body is the poem's visual representation of Gawain's knightly identity's failing. When such identity fails, the body perceptually disaggregates, because it's that identity matrix, that interlocking knot of English Christian chivalric characteristics and behaviors here, that ideally and ever tenuously accords unity to this knightly body in the first place. The chivalric behavior that Gawain performs is so fundamental that without its guarantee of unity he is subject to—or, better, subject of—corporeal disaggregation.

That's what's at stake, I believe, in the exchange of kisses. Gawain has been put in the feminine position in the bedroom; he, further, plants kisses on his host in imitation of the Lady. Such situations thus precipitate the fear of disaggregation: when Gawain acts like a woman, what will happen? The text doesn't wait to find out. The plot hastens to (re)naturalize heterosexuality in the form of a girdle, a "drurye" ("love token" [2033]) from the Lady to Gawain which (she claims) will save him from being hacked to pieces when he faces the Green Knight's ax the following day. In this token, heterosexuality is naturalized as the salvation from disaggregation; it's notable that "drurye" is the same word this poet uses to describe heterosexual sexual relations in Cleanness (699).[35] Further (as also in Pulp Fiction) masculine identity is bought at the expense of the feminine: Gawain fulminates against women when he hears of the plot in which he's been playing (2414–28).

More on that plot later. What matters at this point is that those kisses, however the text attempts to make them mere lip service, can suggest to the queer-minded that solid knightly identity can be split apart without a cataclysmic dissolution: gender, desire, and anatomy here are not, and don't have to be, unified. Gawain kisses Bertilak just like a woman, but he doesn't break like a little girl. The disarticulation of Christian, chivalric identity that emerges as we queerly read these kisses serves to denaturalize for us the very concept of such identity.

Such a denaturalization gives us room to read "against nature": we could read Bertilak's hunt of the "hyndez barayne" (1320) as the masculine version of his wife's hunt of the man; the late medieval discourse of male-male sodomitical relations saw the passive position as a barren feminine one. We could imagine that Bertilak had more agency in this whole plot than he finally admits to Gawain—that his sending his wife in to Gawain was a way of bonding himself, via the woman, to the man. Suppose Morgan's desire to scare Guenevere provided him with a formal cause for his desire to get Gawain. . . . Could this be, then, an example of male-male courtly love, however indirectly expressed? Any such reading that recognizes a positive erotic impulse between Bertilak and Gawain is unthinkable in the culture of this poem, a culture in which erotic kisses between men, not to mention homosexual intercourse, could be considered serious sins; in which, as Michael J. Bennett notes, the relative abundance of young, single, mobile men in Cheshire and Lancashire (the probable location of the poem's audience) was likely to have touched off particular anxieties about homosexual relations— even kisses—because smooth marriage and domestic arrangements and thus inheritance patterns were thereby threatened with disruption;[36] and, further, about whose king's sexual familiarities there were rumors.

The poem undertakes its normalizing project as a project of national import, both in its historical frame (which asserts the Trojan roots of England and seems to hold out that ancient city's fall as a monitory example for contemporary chivalry) and in its apparently relatively close relation to the royal court. Homosexual relations remain unrealized, impossible, a threat to English chivalric identity. No perspective of ecstatic, subversive disaggregation is allowed to Gawain: the poet insists on only one model of identity for him, and that is his armor with its much desired, ever longed-for, but elusive pentangle. But the queer medievalist's use of history suggests other ways to value homosexual relations and the breaking apart of a unified identity. We can indeed read against the "nature" of the text and its context: understanding the history of their containment, we can read the erotic potentials of such kisses between men; we can read the slightly comic tone of such a scene as the head-chopping at Camelot as a potential celebration of new possibilities of bodily powers and satisfactions, and we can see such potential, too, in the body-shattering hunt; we can link such potential to the hint of the Green Knight's cruelty in the Green Chapel scene, and envision another scenario not dominated by medieval Western insistence on unified identity—a scenario in which the shattering of identity and disaggregation of the body can be a much-desired goal.

Michel Foucault's Middle Ages

If *Sir Gawain and the Green Knight* and *Pulp Fiction* recoil from such fragmentation—the movie shunting it into the Middle Ages, but the medieval poem refusing it as well—that scenario is, in fact, the explicitly articulated desire of Michel Foucault. The medieval; sodomy and sadomasochism in male-male relations; the desire for essential identity: the dense cluster of themes I have been tracing isn't unique to the romance genre that informs these medieval and modern narratives. These preoccupations are deeply intertwined in Western culture, in popular fantasy outlets as well as in more analytical and political spheres, such as in Foucault's landmark *History of Sexuality*, Volume One. The coincidence of movie, poem, and book, I contend, is not haphazard; but I want to get at the very significant differences between them. In the rest of this paper I'll look closely at Volume One of Foucault's *History* and support that look with glances at various others of Foucault's works. Generalizations about Foucault's practice of the history of sexuality in Volume One have to be tempered by consideration of Volumes Two and Three, but I'm focusing on Volume One here because it has had the most impact on lesbian and gay studies to date.[37] Foucault's claims about the medieval shifted across the years of reformulating his *History of Sexuality*; and yet, as I shall argue, the pervasive political and ethical dispositions that inform these claims in Volume One persist through his late thought. His use of the medieval—contradictory, nostalgic, and above all tactical—finds possibilities for creativity where *Pulp Fiction* has found shit.

I'm walking something of a tightrope through the course of my analysis here, as I both celebrate Foucault's usefulness and critique aspects of his work. Foucault isn't unassailable; hearkening back to such racial and nationalist agendas as we saw linked to identity formation in *Pulp Fiction* and *SGGK*, for example, Foucault in Volume One uses various eastern civilizations ("China, Japan, India, Rome, the Arabo-Moslem societies" [57]) as uniform, idealized, and unproblematically eroticized societies of the "ars erotica" in order to develop and analyze the concept of the Western "scientia sexualis"—a use so troublingly imperialist that he disavowed it later.[38] What I do want to suggest is that *Pulp Fiction* takes an easy way out of the labyrinth of cultural problems it maps; it is easy at least in part because of its long history—a history that includes the strategies in *SGGK* but which is not inevitable, as Foucault helps us see. My aim is to understand how the all-too-familiar dynamics of a work like *Pulp Fiction* can be exploded and how—instead of the abjection of the inessential and the longing for the pure truth—a new, post-identitarian and post-medieval ethos can be forged.

I'll begin my discussion of Foucault's use of the medieval with one of his famous claims in Volume One of *The History of Sexuality*, the notorious historical distinction between the sodomite and the homosexual. "As defined by the ancient civil or canonical codes," he writes, "sodomy was a category of forbidden acts; their perpetrator was nothing more than the juridical subject of them." But in the late nineteenth century, Foucault goes on, there occurred "an *incorporation of perversions* and a new *specification of individuals*" (42–43, italics in original); so "the sodomite had been a temporary aberration; the homosexual was now a species" (43). Thus David M. Halperin's paradoxical but thoroughly Focauldian proclamation, "[A]lthough there have been, in many different times and places . . . persons who sought sexual contact with other persons of the same sex as themselves, it is only within the last hundred years or so that such persons . . . have been homosexuals."[39] (We might note that this shift finds its counterpart in a shift, at around the same time, that Foucault hypothesizes in *Discipline and Punish*, from the offender to the delinquent. "The delinquent is to be distinguished from the offender by the fact that it is not so much his act as his life that is relevant in characterizing him.")[40] The historical argument about the sodomite has been pursued by Alan Bray and, following him, Jonathan Goldberg, who contend that European Renaissance society, intensely homosocially bonded, is built not only on male social bonds but also on sexual acts unrecognized or unacknowledged as sodomy. Goldberg, in his intricate investigation of the opposition of "acts" to "identities," comments that:

[A]lthough sodomy is, as a sexual act, anything that threatens alliance—any sexual act, that is, that does not promote the aim of married procreative sex . . . and while sodomy involves therefore acts that men might perform with men, women with women . . . , men and women with each other, and anyone with [animals], these acts—or accusations of their performance—emerge into visibility only when those who are said to have done them also can be called traitors, heretics, or the like, at the very least, disturbers of the social order that alliance—marriage arrangements—maintained.[41]

Thus, according to this strand of historical argumentation, men could engage in sexual relations with one another and not only did they not identify themselves as homosexuals, but the acts themselves, part of and continuous with the male-dominated structure of culture, were not even visible as sodomy unless performed in "particularly stigmatizing contexts."[42] Homosexual identity, in contrast, is a sexuality deployed in the process of the subjectivation of modern individuals (the making of subjects, and their domination); in a crucial argument about the nature and operations of modern power, Foucault opposes what he calls the "repressive hypothesis" to his contention that modern power works not merely to repress—to block or negate—but to produce sex, to multiply and implant all forms of it. Modern power constitutes "sex" as the truth—which we tell ourselves is taboo—of each individual: thus sexual, and in particular homosexual, identity.

We can see the applicability of this analysis of modern homosexual identity as we consider Pulp Fiction once again. Though it's clearly a world of male bonding (in this respect picking up from Reservoir Dogs, in which there are no major female characters), sexual relations among men cannot be acknowledged as an inevitable part of the structure of that society. If they could be, it wouldn't be a modern Western culture: thus Mr. Wolf, having detailed and begun to implement a plan to clean up a particularly bloody mess, warns everybody not to congratulate each other too soon: "Let's not start suckin' each other's dicks quite yet" (134), he sneers, the scorn in his statement making it clear that only homos would stop to enjoy this point, taking pleasure when it shouldn't be taken. Homosexual relations are on the horizon of male bonding, but must be kept there. A divide must be erected and anxiously maintained; on the one side are homosexuals, those whose same-sex desires are at the center of their identities; on the other are straight men, whose absence of homosexual desire and aggressive gender style define their identities. The fact that Marsellus has participated in even forced homosexual sex acts must be hidden forever: "Don't tell nobody about this" (108), he orders Butch, lest he be thought a fairy.

Foucault's historically based contrast between the sodomite and the homosexual had a big impact on historical work on sexuality. Scholars of early and late periods took up and ran with this assertion, analyzing what, exactly, sexual identity is, how it's constituted and manifested, whether or not one can indeed talk about sexuality as a constructed core of identity in premodern times. Alongside an increasing number of scholars, I think in fact that any stark opposition is wrong: that is, it's clear from a number of different kinds of sources that men who engaged in acts of male/male sex were known, at least to others if not to themselves, as a specific kind of person and were grouped with others of the same kind.

It may be, indeed, a distortion of the kinds of claims Foucault makes in this introductory Volume One to try to fasten onto an absolute and precise opposition between acts and identities. He specifically refers in this passage to the juridical subject of ancient civil or canonical codes, thus implying that legal identity is what he is talking about at this moment—a sodomite is a person who commits sodomy, just as a traitor is a person who commits treason. In a later piece, a 1982 interview in *Salmagundi* in which references to the Middle Ages are pursued, any starkly-drawn opposition is blurred.[43] No clean conceptual opposition between acts and identities seems to hold absolutely. But a contrast is employed, I argue, in the particular paragraph in Volume One, in the whole volume, and, as I show further on, in much of the later work, for certain *effects*: it provides a structuring principle for Foucault's view of the history—and future—of sexuality. Foucault in Volume One evinces a particular desire for (as he sees it) a premodern realm of clearly apprehensible sexual acts as opposed to the hypocritical and surreptitious world of modern sexual identities. I want to look more closely at Volume One to see, first, what kind of history this is. We can then discern carefully what the medieval is for Foucault, and understand the kind of liberatory potential that is offered by a realm of acts without essential identities—in contrast to the desire for unity expressed in SGGK, for true being in Pulp Fiction.

In looking at Foucault's deployment of the Middle Ages, we must keep in mind that Foucault refuses to write "history" as it has been traditionally formulated. In brief discussions of Foucault's treatment of the Middle Ages, what Pierre Payer has not acknowledged, and what Anne Clark Bartlett has, is Foucault's crucial and thorough assertions of his projects' difference from "history." From Madness and Civilization (1961), through The Order of Things (1966), The Archaeology of Knowledge (1971), and "Nietzsche, Genealogy, History" (1971), to The History of Sexuality (1976–84), he resists the search for determinative origins and "the discourse of the continuous."[44] Yet what makes this anti-historical perspective difficult to keep in mind is the fact that Foucault has also chosen to retain some markers placed by very conventional history, such as "medieval," "modern," and "the rise of the bourgeoisie" (not to mention eras defined by centuries); he retains as well some concepts that derive from totalizing historical analyses ("capital," for one), and some dates that are often taken by conventional historians as watersheds or as moments of origin (1215, for example, the date of the Fourth Lateran Council). That he employs these conventionally accepted historical concepts in his discussion of the repressive hypothesis—that is, that he explicates, via conventional historical markers, a story of causality we moderns tell ourselves, a story that he says is not in itself the whole truth (11)—makes his investment in "history" difficult to ascertain. But as he put it in an interview about Volume One: "I am well aware that I have never written anything but fictions. . . .

One 'fictions' history on the basis of a political reality that makes it true, one 'fictions' a politics not yet in existence on the basis of a historical truth."[45]

The History of Sexuality, Volume One offers a vision of a future politics based on a politically "fictioned" "true" past. And as opposed to the final desire in Pulp Fiction, at the base of Foucault's "fictioned" politics is the inessential identity of its author. Foucault suggests in another Introduction—to The Archaeology of Knowledge—that his writing is a kind of performance, whose gaps and lapses seek the dissolution of his own identity. This Introduction clarifies Foucault's relation to historical markers: he uses them strategically, to clear a space ("this blank space from which I speak") for his own project.[46] It is precisely his tactical deployment of history that provides the space of his self-annihilation and of his future politics of disaggregation. How, exactly, Foucault uses the conventionally delineated Middle Ages in his project of disaggregating identity is the issue to which I now turn.

In Volume One Foucault posits (by using conventional markers) two major historical "ruptures," shifts in the history of sexuality mapped, as he puts it, as the history of "mechanisms of repression": one in the seventeenth century, one in the twentieth:

> The first . . . was characterized by the advent of the great prohibitions, the exclusive promotion of adult marital sexuality, the imperatives of decency, the obligatory concealment of the body, the reduction to silence and mandatory reticences of language. The second . . . was really less a rupture than an inflexion of the curve: this was the moment when the mechanisms of repression were seen as beginning to loosen their grip. . . . (115)

"The chronology of the techniques [of repression] themselves goes back," he notes with a characteristically broad stroke, "a long way." Making this dating more precise, he goes on: "Their point of formation must be sought in the penitential practices of medieval Christianity or, rather in the dual series" of changes imposed by the Fourth Lateran Council of 1215 and then by devotional practices of the sixteenth century (115–16). We might ask, for starters, what Foucault gains in adhering to a paradigm of ruptures and periods, particularly since the points of rupture seem so constantly revised, so labyrinthine (note the "or rather" in this passage, and such revisions throughout the book). This is the whole (ruptured) style of his Nietzschean model of effective history, of course.[47] But it might also be read as itself having a specific rhetorical effect; perhaps it affords him what early in Volume One he calls "the speaker's benefit": the verbal act of speaking of a time before "the great prohibitions" puts the speaker prophetically outside of or beyond them, and thus "anticipates the coming freedom" (6). Foucault's analysis of the discourse of liberation (the ruse of the repressive hypothesis) can, I suggest, be applied to his own use of the Middle Ages in "a discourse that combines the fervor of knowledge, the determination to change the laws, and the longing for the garden of earthly delights" (7). I'll pick up on such longing for past delights in a moment.

But notice first what role the medieval period plays in this passage about the two major historical ruptures: it is the time period in which techniques of modern subjectivation took form. Specifically, the medieval is the time in which, after 1215, the obligation of annual confession began the process of putting sex into discourse (a process completed by the seventeenth century [20]). The Middle Ages here is the time of the seeds of modern "men's subjection: their constitution as subjects in both senses of the word" (60); "Since the Middle Ages at least," Foucault contends, confession has been a mainstay of such subjection; the Christian pastoral made sex an "enigma," creating "modern societies" who speak and exploit sex as "the secret" (35). Further, Foucault claims that modern power's suppression of its own actual multiplicity originated in the Middle Ages (86). And even if these "beginnings" of modern sexual subjectivity were "surreptitious," they were "long ago . . . already making" themselves "felt at the time of the Christian pastoral of the flesh" (156)—already long in evidence before the sixteenth century.

Thus there is a powerful and continuous use of the Middle Ages in Volume One as the site of the beginnings of modern sexual subject formation. I'm not going to evaluate Foucault's particular claims about the institution of confession here; my intent is only to present his general claims about periodization.[48] And what I find in general counterpoint to this pervasive use of the Middle Ages is another use, wherein the Middle Ages forms the firm border between us moderns and a very different age with very different systems of codes governing sexual practices: codes that center sexual practices on matrimonial relations, that still determine "nature" as a kind of law, and that do not differentiate the concept of the "unnatural" into a specific field of sexuality (37–39). It was a time, this theme goes, of a "markedly unitary" discourse ("un discours assez fortement unitaire" [46]) around "the theme of the flesh and the practice of penance," a uniformity that was "broken apart" ("décomposée" [46]) more recently (33). At this point I hear something like a note of nostalgia tuning Foucault's historical song.

Such nostalgia is even more audible in the claim that "little by little, the nakedness of the questions formulated by the confession manuals of the Middle Ages, and a good number of those still in use in the seventeenth century, was veiled" (18). Foucault argues that increasing discretion of early modern confessors was advised, so that less detail would be articulated: no longer was there, as he puts it, a complete "description of the respective positions of the partners, the postures assumed, gestures, places touched, caresses, the precise moment of pleasure—an entire painstaking review of the sexual act in its very unfolding" (19). In his style that mimes the rhythms of the medieval confession itself, Foucault seems here to assert that medieval language was able to record so precisely as itself to mime "the sexual act in its very unfolding" ("dans son opération même" [27]). It's difficult to pin down the historical value or even the place in his own argument of Foucault's idealizing assertion here.[49] This description in Volume One, which Foucault offers as an *accurate* account of modern power (the beginning of the proliferative modern process of putting sex into discourse) sounds much like the mocking description of the repressive hypothesis that opens the volume: "it would seem" ("dit-on" [9]), he writes in the opening, that the beginning of the seventeenth century was still "a time of direct gestures, shameless discourse, and open transgressions, when anatomies were shown and intermingled at will, and knowing children hung about amid the laughter of adults: it was a period when bodies 'made a display of themselves'" (3). Is this time of direct gestures, easy contact between body parts, and naked descriptions of nakedness a rhetorical effect or genealogical-historical fact? (More generally, and hearkening back to my earlier observation about the repressive hypothesis: is this repressive hypothesis a story Foucault must tell to produce a certain modernity, or one he believes we moderns really believe?) Following his comments on politics, fictioning, and history, I think both propositions are true: the Middle Ages plays a role in the history of sexuality formulated around the mechanisms of repression—the period works for his effective history, he deploys it for certain effects; *and* he believes, or at least desires, that it really was like that.

Now it may be that these two perspectives on the Middle Ages—seen as a period that produces our modernity, and as a period quite separate and different from our own—are conceptually coherent, part of a whole genealogical approach to the modern subject. The demonstration of modern contingency traces the forces that produce us and at the same time suggests that we can be different in the future because we were not always like this. But I do not want to harmonize these two strains completely and thus elide not only the obviously strategic use of the

Middle Ages in Volume One but also—crucially—the desire that emerges from this contradictory history. Central to discerning the value of this double position is in fact that nostalgic tone; various critics have noted an idealization and have assigned varying importance to it. Medievalists have always taken exception to a Middle Ages that functions "as a lost and golden age," as Bartlett puts it; yet I don't want to discard utopianism altogether.[50] The utopian, the elegaic, what I've been calling the nostalgic, functions as part of a serious ethical and aesthetic vision of the present and the future: a view of political reality informs Foucault's historical pronouncement about the sodomite and the homosexual, and, in turn, the historical pronouncement allows Foucault to fiction a future politics.

Foucault has insisted that he doesn't study historically distant periods in order to find an alternative to the present: "I am not looking for an alternative; you can't find the solution of a problem in the solution of another problem raised at another moment by other people." Indeed, he maintains, "There is no exemplary value in a period which is not our period . . . it is not anything to get back to";[51] and yet historical analysis, he comments, can be useful in showing us that, and perhaps how, such a "fictitious unity" (Volume One, 154) as modern sexuality can be broken apart and reconfigured. Foucault uses the opposition of acts to identity, surface to depth, premodernity to modernity, in order to show that future sexuality does not have to be dominated by current notions of identity. The potential for acts (not entailed with identity) to shatter the modern liberal subject is great; insofar as such a category of acts is associated with the premodern in his historiography, Foucault expresses a desire for the premodern.

What I find in Foucault's work, carried through the late interviews, is not only an analytical focus on the body as imprintable surface (as everyone sees)[52] but a desire—which is mistakenly reduced to *mere* nostalgia—for a realm of clearly apprehensible acts

and legible surfaces. In *Discipline and Punish* the premodern offender's acts were clearly motivated by "a free, conscious will,"
Foucault writes, while the modern delinquent's internal "in-
stincts, drives, tendencies, character" muddy the surface (253).
In the Middle Ages invoked in the 1980 Introduction to *Herculine
Barbin*, the hermaphroditic body is clearly legible, not clouded
over by the necessity of interpretation.[53] At the beginning of *The
History of Sexuality*, Volume One, the scene opens on "this bright
day" (3) ["ce plein jour" (9)] of bodies displayed and accessible,
on the surface and without mediation. And at the end of Volume
One, Foucault calls for a resistance to coercive modern "sexuality" and its "fictitious unity" in order to "counter the grips of
power with the claims of bodies, pleasures, and knowledges"
(157)—calls, as Leo Bersani puts it, for a "reinventing of the
body as a surface of multiple sources of pleasure."[54] There is an
emphasis on the visible and apparent, on the apprehensible in its
immediacy; it even sounds "prediscursive," as Judith Butler
points out, despite Foucault's "official" line that (as she puts it)
"there is no 'sex' in itself"—and certainly no body—"which is
not produced by complex interactions of discourse and power."[55]
This pre- or extra-discursive reinvention project has as its basis
"desexualization," as Foucault put it in an interview published at
about the time of Volume One's publication: a reinvention "with
the body, with its elements, its surfaces, its volumes, its depths,
[of] a nondisciplinary eroticism: that of a body in a volatile and
diffuse state given to chance encounters and incalculable pleasures" not centered on genitalia.[56] Foucault suggests in a 1978
interview, "Le Gai savoir," that in anonymous sexual encounters
there is "an exceptional possibility of desubjectivization, of desubjection, perhaps not the most radical but in any case suf-
ficiently intense to be worth taking note of. . . . It's not the
affirmation of identity that's important, it's the affirmation of
non-identity": the act, the surface, and the loss of identity are
linked.[57] The body is turned inside out; its depths become sur-

faces; this body is "diffuse," "exploding,"[58] and without the old hierarchical conceptualizations of internal drives and impulses.

In the second and third volumes of *The History of Sexuality* as well as in late discussions in the gay press, Foucault's emphasis on *becoming* rather than on *being*, performance rather than ontology, is marked; in studying the "arts of existence" in Volume Two, for example, Foucault clarifies that he means "those intentional and voluntary actions by which men not only set themselves rules of conduct, but also seek to transform themselves, to change themselves in their singular being, and to make their life into an *oeuvre*" (10). Finally, recalling to us the very different treatment we've seen in *Pulp Fiction*, Foucault happily links such an acts-centered disposition against depth to sadomasochism in a 1982 interview: "I think that S/M . . . [is] the real creation of new possibilities of pleasure. . . . The idea that S/M is related to a deep violence, that S/M practice is a way of liberating this violence, this aggression, is stupid." And in the same interview, he links S/M to the "strategic game" of medieval "'courtly love.'"[59]

But the valorization of surfaces and thus clearly apprehensible acts needs to be considered carefully. "Acts" cannot be imagined to be immediately self-apparent. Foucault, genealogist, is of course entirely aware of this. Earlier, in *Discipline and Punish*, he suggests that the modern penal state itself problematizes the notion of a proven and punishable act (19). At specific moments in Volume One, too (elaborated in Volume Two [e.g., 92]), Foucault makes perfectly clear the complexities of judging acts, especially in the Christian tradition. In his discussion of the expansion of the scope of confession in Volume One, for example, he notes that an "evolution tended to make the flesh into the root of all evil, shifting the most important moment of transgression from the act itself to the stirrings—so difficult to perceive and formulate—of desire" (19–20). Here I assume that what's referred to, the Biblical precedent for this shift, is Matthew 5:28, Christ's warning in his Sermon on the Mount: "But I say unto you, That whosoever looketh on a woman to lust after her hath committed adultery with her already in his heart" (King James Version); the act, that is, has already taken place even before the act has occurred. This is a deconstruction of the act pursued with moral vigor by patristic writers such as Saint Augustine and Saint Jerome.[60]

Further problematizing the concept: what we see "in the act," in its "concrete realization" (Volume Two, 63), on the surface, does not necessarily indicate—and certainly does not exhaust—its social meaning or function. Again, Foucault, committed to explicating the ways power infuses and saturates the body from the interior, would never "officially" argue that it does; but the opposition he offers between acts and identities sets up a field (acts) that is not in itself historically and conceptually nuanced enough to register differences in social empowerment. The problem, at this point, is less in Foucault's schematic remarks in the introductory Volume One than in the sometimes reductive directions in which scholars have taken them. To see the analytical limitations I'm suggesting here, let's return to SGGK, whose representation of sexual interrelations provides a clear example of the necessity of interpreting acts in relation to prior chains of acts of which they are citations, to conventions of meaning, and particularly to existent structures of power.

Thus far in my analysis of the medieval poem I've traced the textual production and obviation of the possibility of sex between Gawain and Bertilak, arguing that the threat to Gawain's identity posed in the seduction scene and in male same-sex eroticism precipitates a vision of bodily disaggregation, a threat to unified identity which is ultimately contained by the poem. But what's really startling in SGGK is the poem's revelation, very late and via an apparently gratuitous and contradictory detail, that these men are actually tokens in a plot between women—a shadowy but terrifying plot of intensely desired vengeance between Morgan la Faye and Guenevere. Gawain's acts are significant not only as they play out a straight chivalric masculine identity, but also as they play out a female female desire. Remember again the narrative: Bertilak, Gawain's host at Hautdesert, is the Green Knight, that verdant weirdo who rode into Camelot a year before on his green horse and challenged the court to a beheading game. This strange fact of the Green Knight's identity is revealed to Gawain after the beheading ordeal at the Green Chapel is finally over. The ordeal itself has not gone as Gawain has expected: after feigning twice, the Green Knight finally delivers the blow Gawain has anticipated—dreaded—for a year, a checked blow that just nicks him slightly. In explanation, the Green Knight reveals that he himself is Bertilak and that the seduction at his castle has not only proceeded according to his design but also is correlated with the initial plot that started Gawain's adventure in the first place: at Camelot, the Green Knight challenged Gawain to chop his head off, after which he a year later would chop off Gawain's. Now Gawain learns that because he accepted the girdle at Hautdesert and did not exchange it, as agreed earlier, with Bertilak (after two sinless days of seduction), he receives a wound from the Green Knight, the little "nirt," on the third swing.

As if this weren't intricate and surprising enough, Bertilak then reveals that his wife's companion at the castle is in fact Morgan la Faye, who is responsible for the entire adventure. The far-flung design—to send Bertilak to Camelot in the shape of a green knight to accomplish three things (to test the renown of the Round Table, to drive Arthur's court out of their minds, and to scare Guenevere to death)—was *Morgan's*. Bertilak's rhetoric here, including those three reasons for Morgan's plotting, suggests that the first two reasons he mentions—that she wanted to "test the quality" (or, in an alternative translation, "attack the arrogance"[61]) of the Round Table and that she wanted to deprive them of their senses—are auxiliary to the final reason, given much more narrative time: that Morgan wanted to grieve

Guenevere mortally, to make her suffer and die. As he says to
Gawain:

> Ho wayned me vpon þis wyse to your wynne halle
> For to assay þe surquidré, 3if hit soth were
> Þat rennes of þe grete renoun of þe Rounde Table;
> Ho wayned me þis wonder your wyttez to reue,
> For to haf greued Gaynour and gart hir to dy3e
> With glopnyng of þat ilke gome þat gostlych speked
> With his hede in his honde bifore þe hy3e table.
>
> (2456–62)

In Borroff's translation:

> She guided me in this guise to your glorious hall,
> To assay, if such it were, the surfeit of pride
> That is rumored of the retinue of the Round Table.
> She put this shape upon me to puzzle your wits,
> To afflict the fair queen, and frighten her to death
> With awe of that elvish man that eerily spoke
> With his head in his hand before the high table.[62]

The word "glopnyng" to describe Guenevere's intended response
is key here: Borroff has translated it as "awe," but, as Douglas M.
Moon comments, the best definition of the term "would be one
that lies somewhere between terror and depression," suggesting "a somewhat more protracted process than instantaneous
death."[63] Morgan wants to produce a lingering and lasting effect;
maybe the best rendering would be that Morgan wants to "get at"
or "get to" or just "get" Guenevere—terminally. The fact that she
doesn't succeed paradoxically extends her relation to the Queen,
gives her in fact further chances to get her.

  Almost every reader forgets Bertilak's comments here, forgets
that the whole plot of SGGK is in fact instigated by Morgan. This is
no accident, not some mass distraction on the part of all of the
poem's readers; it's the poem's doing, of course. With fewer than

one hundred lines to go, the poem explains the greenness of the knight and the head-chopping at Camelot, giving a reason that is reassuringly traditional: Morgan, tutored by Merlin, is pursuing her old animosity against Guenevere. According to the Prose *Lancelot*, Morgan hated Guenevere more than any other woman in the world, and had from the time they first met; this was because Morgan fell in love with Guiomar, Guenevere's nephew, and Guenevere, coming upon them in bed, convinced her nephew to give up Morgan.[64] But traditional or not, this explanation—as many readers, most notably Sheila Fisher, have remarked—seems inadequate to the major actions and ostensible preoccupations of *SGGK*.[65] Bertilak has, after all, already claimed his agency in the seduction, and declared that the ultimate purpose of the action was the moral testing of Gawain. What, then, does Morgan's plot explain? It's neither correlated with the rest of the narrative nor followed out. Why is Morgan adduced at all? Why bring her up in the first place?

I suggest that this narrative gesture, like the production of a logical possibility of homosexual relations between Bertilak and Gawain I analyzed earlier, is the poem's move of adducing homosexual relations only in order to deny the possibility, to render them incoherent: this motivation is unnecessary, in excess of the narrative. If we read that incoherence as a touch of textual queerness, something that doesn't make sense according to the explicit heteronormative standards of romance plotting, we'll uncover an embarrassing truth—a truth embarrassing to the whole genre's ostensible commitment to straightness: this romance is more fundamentally concerned with—structured by—same-sex bonds than opposite-sex ones.[66] I argue that if one powerful potential motive in *SGGK* (never realized, never allowed by the text to flower) is male-male eroticism, there is an even more deeply buried plot, profound and hidden, in which Gawain is a pawn—between women.

Homosexual acts between men are more obviously, while still implicitly, suggested in this poem than are those between the women: acts between women, in fact, can only be figured as shadowy and terrifying even (and only) in potentia. This is a significant difference: women's acts are not recorded, not codified as fully as men's because women don't act in medieval public spheres as do men. The same thing goes for differences in the possibilities that acts by racially marginalized people or those from non-literate classes can and will be recorded and codified. The point, then, is that "acts," as an analytical category, cannot in itself be regarded as sufficient and self-explanatory.[67] As feminist scholars have continually insisted we ask, "Who can act, when, and under what circumstances?"

The Foucauldian distinction between identity and act has, however, proven immensely fruitful in current queer political organizing. The importance for current activist practice of Volume One is immense: David M. Halperin observes in Saint Foucault, on the basis of an unsystematic 1990 survey of people active in ACT UP/New York in the late '80s, that "the single most important intellectual source of political inspiration for contemporary AIDS activists—at least for the more theoretically-minded or better-outfitted among them" is Volume One of the History of Sexuality.[68] Just as an analytical model of sex acts challenges models of identity, so does a model of political acts: current queer resistance to identity politics is informed, I think, by an acts-centered model of coalition politics that picks up on Foucault's preference for acts; there is a focus on performativity, on performance, and on visibility, in what Heather Findlay has recently called "a politics of the signifier."[69] Such an acts-centered model is politically efficacious in particular circumstances, countering the persecution of already marginalized identity-based groups—efficacious when, for example, the concept of "high risk acts" in AIDS activist discourse counters the phobic, racist, and misogynist concept of "high risk groups." But queer politics can constantly benefit from feminist tutelage, as the connotations of the term "queer" themselves suggest (still young, white, and male): who gets to act—and who gets to act up?[70]

The very concept of self-identical and thus self-apparent acts apprehensible via the surface, then, needs to be nuanced in scholarly and in activist practice. The refusal of a depth model of identity does not require that we take acts at face value but that we de-couple acts from essentialized identities and that we read them in terms of constitutive contexts. Identities may be constituted by acts—the theory of nonessentialized, performative identity so fully enunciated in *Gender Trouble* has conceptual roots in Foucault's genealogy of modern sexual identity in Volume One, and Volume One in turn continues to perform the dissolution of essential identity that we saw in the Preface to *The Archaeology of Knowledge*—but acts are not themselves fully self-identical or self-apparent.

From a conventional historicist point of view, Foucault's locating self-apparent acts in the Middle Ages in Volume One of *The History of Sexuality* might seem both essentializing and nostalgic. Essentializing it is not, as I've just suggested. Furthermore, nostalgia isn't what it used to be. Foucault, tactical, forward-looking, and resistant, is fictioning history on the basis of a political reality that makes it true, in order that he can fiction a politics not yet in existence. Sexual identity now is constructed as truth, so that only in resistance to modern sexual subjectivation is there any possibility of reinvention or "explosion" of the body into surface. In contrast to the medieval in *Pulp Fiction*, then, that space of abjection and otherness—the space where sodomy, S/M, southerners, and blacks get dumped in the creation of a unified, straight, white masculinity—and in contrast to what I see in the medieval *SGGK* threatening a cataclysmic dissolution of identity, the Middle Ages Foucault most deeply desires is a time whose lack of unified sexuality is preferable to the present with its "fictitious unity" of normative heterosexuality, a time whose sexual disaggregation is not to be feared but can in the modern day offer a creative, even liberatory, potential. "There is a creation of anarchy within the body," Foucault comments in a 1975 interview suggesting such disaggregation, "where its hierarchies, its localizations and designations, its organicity, if you will, are in the process of disintegrating. . . . This is something 'unnameable,' 'useless,' outside of all the programs of desire. It is the body made totally plastic by pleasure: something that opens itself, that tightens, that throbs, that beats, that gapes."[71] Here is that prediscursive body gaping wide open.

So when Hayden White analyzes, and goes on to condemn, Foucault's historiography as "all surface," I can agree with the terms of the analysis but value them entirely differently.[72] "Of course," states Ed Cohen on this late material, "Foucault does not characterize these new possibilities of pleasure as inherently 'political' or 'resistant'";[73] thus his qualification, for example, of the radicality of anonymous sexual encounters (quoted above). But he does place them at the center of any future deliberations of the "homosexual movement" about the organization of a given society. And we can link such a project of desexualization, disaggregation into surfaces, to a feminist project (as I've been suggesting) of transforming the "social relations within which sexuality is organized and articulated," as Biddy Martin puts it.[74] So that finally, instead of negatively viewing the concept of disaggregation as a dehumanizing desubjection, as does Gawain in *SGGK*; or desiring a turn from an impure and inessential identity to some solidity guaranteed by God, as does Jules in *Pulp Fiction*—and instead of considering such a desire an inevitability, as the normalizing structures operant in those texts clearly do—we can choose to be tutored by an aesthetic and ethical practice, after Foucault, of becoming rather than being. In this context, getting medieval is the best we can do.[75]

Notes

1. Quentin Tarantino, *Pulp Fiction: A Quentin Tarantino Screenplay* (New York: Hyperion, 1994, p.108. Copyright 1994, Quentin Tarantino. Reprinted with permission by Hyperion. All references to *Pulp Fiction* are to this screenplay ("scr" before a page reference in my text incates non-dialogue material).

2. Todd McCarthy, "*Pulp Fiction*," *Variety*, 23 May 1994, 9; Courtney Love, interview with Kevin Sessums, "Love Child," *Vanity Fair*, June 1995, 106–15, 169–71. Tarantino's earlier work in *Reservoir Dogs* "spoke to Kurt Cobain" (according to another *Vanity Fair* article quoted by J. Hoberman in "Pulp and Glory," *Village Voice*, 11 October 1994, 61, 75 at 61).

3. "Idol Threats: Bastards!" *Film Threat* 20 (February 1995): 20.

4. Richard Corliss, "Saturday Night Fever," *Time*, 6 June 1994, 73.

5. *Li Livres de jostice et de plet*, ed. Pierre Rapetti (Paris: Didot Frères, 1850), 18.24.22 (pp. 279–80), documents this law from the legal school of Orléans c. 1270: "Cil qui sont sodomite prové doivent perdre les c . . . [sic]. Et se il le fet segonde foiz, il doit perdre menbre. Et se il le fet la tierce foiz, il doit estre ars." ("He who has been proved to be a sodomite must lose his testicles. And if he does it a second time, he must lose his member. And if he does it a third time, he must be burned," trans. Louis Crompton, "The Myth of Lesbian Impunity: Capital Laws from 1270 to 1791," *Historical Perspectives on Homosexuality*, special issue of *The Journal of Homosexuality* 6.1–2 [1980–81]: 11–25, at 13.) See John Boswell, *Christianity, Social Tolerance, and Homosexuality* (Chicago and London: University of Chicago Press, 1980); James A. Brundage, *Law, Sex, and Christian Society in Medieval Europe* (Chicago and London: University of Chicago Press, 1987); and Crompton for discussion of sodomy and other sexual legislation throughout the Western medieval period.

6. Dir. Don Siegel, Universal Pictures, 1973. I thank Alfred Arteaga for this cinematic lore.

7. Janet Maslin, "Quentin Tarantino's Wild Ride on Life's Dangerous Road," *The New York Times*, 23 September 1994, C1, C34, at C34.

8. Anthony Lane, "Degrees of Cool," *The New Yorker*, 10 October 1994, 95–97, at 96.

9. See Sharon Willis, "The Fathers Watch the Boys' Room," *Camera Obscura* 32 (1993–94): 40–73, for an analysis of the thematics of shit in

Tarantino's three screenplays (*Reservoir Dogs*, *True Romance*, and *Pulp Fiction*), particularly its relation to anal sex, race, and history.

10. *Sleep With Me*, dir. Rory Kelly, August Entertainment, 1994; *Reservoir Dogs*, dir. Quentin Tarantino, Miramax, 1992. See bell hooks, "Cool Tool," and Robin Wood, "Slick Shtick," in the March 1995 *Artforum* discussion of the film, "Pulp the Hype: On the Q.T." (62–67, 108–10), for observations on *Pulp Fiction*'s relation to *Reservoir Dogs*. Tarantino "agrees with the suggestion that he's able to throw gay and gay-ish references into his work because his generation is cool with the subject" (Steve Warren, "Gay 'Top Gun'? A Talk with Tarantino," San Francisco *Sentinel*, 12 October 1994, 33). In *Pulp Fiction*, I would argue, "the subject" is thrown in only to try to demonstrate (and cash in on) mainstream white-boy "coolness."

11. John J. Winkler, *The Constraints of Desire: The Anthropology of Sex and Gender in Ancient Greece* (New York and London: Routledge, 1990), 54–64. I owe this phrase to Will Roscoe, "Strange Craft, Strange History, Strange Folks: Cultural Amnesia and the Case for Lesbian and Gay Studies," *American Anthropologist* 97 (1995): 448–53.

12. See Marc Steyn in *The Spectator*, 22 October 1994, 60–61.

13. See Willis, "The Fathers Watch"; Lee Edelman, "Tearooms and Sympathy, or, The Epistemology of the Water Closet," in *The Lesbian and Gay Studies Reader*, ed. Henry Abelove, Michèle Aina Barale, and David M. Halperin (New York and London: Routledge, 1993), 553–74, discusses the problematics of shitting in the context of 1960s national security in the U.S.

14. See "Quentin Tarantino on *Pulp Fiction*, as told to Manohla Dargis," *Sight and Sound*, November 1994, 16–19, at 17.

15. hooks, "Cool Tool," 108.

16. Dennis Cooper, "Minor Magic," *Artforum*, March 1995, 66.

17. hooks, "Cool Tool," 65–66.

18. Willis, "The Fathers Watch," 62.

19. hooks, "Cool Tool," 66.

20. Willis, "The Fathers Watch," observes the significance of the "flesh" color of Marsellus's Band-Aid (49). The image of the black woman appears for a moment in the movie but not in the published screenplay. See Willis, 56–67.

21. Umberto Eco, *Travels in Hyperreality: Essays*, trans. William Weaver (San Diego/San Diego: Harcourt Brace Jovanovich, 1986), 72. I owe this

reference to Elizabeth Scala, in her formal response to an earlier version of this paper.

22. Eco, *Travels*, 64–65.

23. I pursue this formulation in "Chaucer's Queer Touches/A Queer Touches Chaucer," *Exemplaria* 7 (1995): 75–92, esp. 86–87.

24. *Le Lai de Lanval*, ed. Jean Rychner, Textes Littéraires Français (Geneva: Droz, 1958), ll. 274–302; *Eneas: Roman du XIIe siècle*, ed. J. J. Salverda de Grave, 2 vols. (Paris: Champion, 1925–29), 2:8566–76, 2: 9130–70. On the *Eneas*, see William Burgwinkle, "Knighting the Classical Hero: Homo/Hetero Affectivity in *Eneas*," *Exemplaria* 7 (1993):1–43.

25. H. Oskar Sommer, *The Vulgate Version of the Arthurian Romances*, 8 vols. (Washington, D.C.: Carnegie Institute, 1908–16), 4:143–46. I owe this point to Robert L. A. Clark's excellent unpublished paper, "The Courtly and the Queer: Some Like It Not," 1995.

26. See Michael J. Bennett, "The Court of Richard II and the Promotion of Literature," in *Chaucer's England: Literature in Social Context*, ed. Barbara Hanawalt (Minneapolis: University of Minnesota Press, 1992), 3–20; and see D. W. Robertson, Jr., "The Concept of Courtly Love as an Impediment to the Understanding of Medieval Texts," *Essays in Medieval Culture* (Princeton: Princeton University Press, 1980), 257–72, esp. 266–67, for a discussion of *SGGK* as a "warning to all Englishmen," via its use of the fall of Troy.

27. This analysis of *SGGK* rehearses the analysis in my article, "A Kiss Is Just a Kiss: Heterosexuality and Its Consolations in *Sir Gawain and the Green Knight*," *diacritics* 24.2–3 (1994): 205–26. All quotations of *SGGK* are from the second edition, edited by Norman Davis, of *Sir Gawain and the Green Knight*, ed. J. R. R. Tolkien and E. V. Gordon (Oxford: Clarendon, 1967). Translations of the Middle English are mine unless otherwise noted, informed by the notes and glosses in Malcolm Andrew and Ronald Waldron, eds., *The Poems of the Pearl Manuscript*, York Medieval Texts, 2nd ser. (Berkeley and Los Angeles: University of California Press, 1982), and influenced by Marie Borroff, trans., *Sir Gawain and the Green Knight* (New York: Norton, 1967).

28. Glenn Burger, "Kissing the Pardoner," *PMLA* 107 (1992): 1143–56, esp. 1153n6.

29. See Geraldine Heng, "Feminine Knots and the Other *Sir Gawain and the Green Knight*," *PMLA* 106 (1991): 500–14, for a discussion of the pen-

tangle in this vein. See also Heng, "A Woman Wants: The Lady, *Gawain*, and the Forms of Seduction," *Yale Journal of Criticism* 5 (1992): 101–34; Sheila Fisher, "Leaving Morgan Aside: Women, History, and Revisionism in *Sir Gawain and the Green Knight*," *The Passing of Arthur*, ed. Christopher Baswell and William Sharpe (New York and London: Garland Publishing, 1988), 129–51; and Fisher, "Taken Men and Token Women in *Sir Gawain and the Green Knight*," in *Seeking the Woman in Late Medieval and Renaissance Writings*, ed. Sheila Fisher and Janet E. Halley (Knoxville: University of Tennessee Press, 1989), 71–105.

30. Fisher, "Taken Men and Token Women," 78.

31. See Laura Hibbard Loomis, *Adventures in the Middle Ages: A Memorial Collection of Essays and Studies* (New York: Burt Franklin, 1962), 300, citing George Lyman Kittredge, *A Study of Gawain and the Green Knight* (Cambridge, MA, 1916), 79ff., on such analogues to *SGGK*.

32. See Heng, "A Woman Wants," 116.

33. See Louise Olga Fradenburg, *City, Marriage, Tournament: Arts of Rule in Late Medieval Scotland* (Madison and London: University of Wisconsin Press, 1991), esp. 192–224, on the "phenomenological crisis" that is knighthood.

34. See Davis, ed., *Gawain*, xxi.

35. Robert J. Menner, ed., *Purity*, Yale Studies in English 61 (1920; repr. Hamden, CT: Archon, 1970).

36. See Michael J. Bennett, *Community, Class and Careerism: Cheshire and Lancashire in the Age of Sir Gawain and the Green Knight* (Cambridge: Cambridge University Press, 1983).

37. *The History of Sexuality Volume I, An Introduction*, trans. Robert Hurley (New York: Pantheon, 1978); originally published as *La Volonté de savoir* (Paris: Gallimard, 1976). *The Use of Pleasure*, trans. Robert Hurley (New York: Pantheon, 1985); originally published as *L'Usage des plaisirs* (Paris: Gallimard, 1984). *The Care of the Self*, trans. Robert Hurley (New York: Pantheon, 1986); originally published as *Le Souci de soi* (Paris: Gallimard, 1984). I include the French when my analysis depends on more precise usage and the English translation is slightly loose.

38. See "On the Genealogy of Ethics: An Overview of Work in Progress," *The Foucault Reader*, ed. Paul Rabinow (New York: Pantheon, 1984), 340–72, esp. 347–48. See also Ann Laura Stoler, *Race and the Education of Desire: Foucault's History of Sexuality and the Colonial Order of Things* (Durham:

Duke University Press, 1995), 6, who poses the acute question: "What happens to Foucault's chronologies when the technologies of sexuality are refigured in an imperial field?"

39. David M. Halperin, *One Hundred Years of Homosexuality and Other Essays on Greek Love* (New York and London: Routledge, 1990), 29.

40. Michel Foucault, *Discipline and Punish: The Birth of the Prison*, trans. Alan Sheridan (New York: Pantheon, 1978), 251; originally published as *Surveiller et punir: Naissance de la prison* (Paris: Gallimard, 1975).

41. Jonathan Goldberg, *Sodometries: Renaissance Texts, Modern Sexualities* (Stanford: Stanford University Press, 1992), 19.

42. Goldberg, *Sodometries*, 19.

43. "Sexual Choice, Sexual Act: An Interview with Michel Foucault," trans. James O'Higgins, *Salmagundi* 58–59 (1982–83): 10–24.

44. Pierre Payer, "Foucault on Penance and the Shaping of Sexuality," *Studies in Religion* 14 (1985): 313–20; Anne Clark Bartlett, "Foucault's 'Medievalism,'" *Mystics Quarterly* 20 (1994): 10–18; Foucault, "Introduction," *The Archaeology of Knowledge*, in *The Archaeology of Knowledge and the Discourse on Language*, trans. A. M. Sheridan Smith and Rupert Swyer (New York: Pantheon, 1972), 12.

45. "The History of Sexuality," interview with Lucette Finas, trans. Leo Marshall, in *Power/Knowledge: Selected Interviews and Other Writings 1972–1977*, ed. Colin Gordon (New York: Pantheon, 1980), 183–93, at 193.

46. Foucault, *The Archaeology of Knowledge*, 17. John Mowitt's unpublished manuscript, "Queer Resistance: Foucault and *The Unnamable*," comments usefully on Foucault's performativity. See also the section, "Performing Foucault," in Eve Kosofsky Sedgwick, "Gender Criticism," in *Redrawing the Boundaries: The Transformation of English and American Literary Studies*, ed. Stephen Greenblatt and Giles Gunn (New York: MLA, 1992), 271–302, esp. 285–91.

47. "Nietzsche, Genealogy, History," in *Language, Counter-Memory, Practice: Selected Essays and Interviews*, ed. Donald F. Bouchard, trans. Donald F. Bouchard and Sherry Simon (Ithaca: Cornell University Press, 1977), 139–64, esp. 154–57.

48. For contrasting analyses of Foucault's claims concerning confession see Pierre Payer, "Foucault on Penance," and Gregory W. Gross, "Secret Rules: Sex, Confession, and Truth in *Sir Gawain and the Green Knight*," *Arthuriana* 4 (1994): 146–74.

49. See Bartlett, "Foucault's 'Medievalism,'" 15, for other moments of linguistic nostalgia in Foucault's works.

50. Bartlett castigates what she sees as "Foucault's view of the Middle Ages as a sort of utopian realm, which offers a cultural space free of the routine and disabling surveillance that, for Foucault, characterizes modern society" ("Foucault's 'Medievalism,'" 15). Eve Kosofsky Sedgwick finds "utopian or elegaic elements," but sees them as "fugitive" ("Gender Criticism," 280).

51. Foucault, "On the Genealogy of Ethics," 343 and 347.

52. See, for example, Judith Butler, *Gender Trouble: Feminism and the Subversion of Identity* (New York: Routledge, 1990), 134–39.

53. *Herculine Barbin: Being the Recently Discovered Memoirs of a Nineteenth-Century French Hermaphrodite*, trans. Richard McDougall (New York: Pantheon, 1980), vii–xvii. See Arnold Davidson, "Sex and the Emergence of Sexuality," *Critical Inquiry* 14 (1987): 16–48, esp. 19, on Foucault's simplifications of medieval and early modern legal, religious, and medical treatment of hermaphrodites; and Lorraine Daston and Katharine Park, "Hermaphrodites in Renaissance France," *Critical Matrix: Princeton Working Papers in Women's Studies* 1 (1985): 1–19, esp. 3, 6–7.

54. Bersani, "Is the Rectum a Grave?" in *AIDS: Cultural Analysis, Cultural Activism*, ed. Douglas Crimp (Cambridge, MA: MIT Press, 1988), 197–222, at 219. See also *Homos* (Cambridge, MA: Harvard University Press, 1995), at 81. Note that Bersani takes issue with what he sees as Foucault's turn away from sex acts (in "Is the Rectum a Grave?") and with Foucault's description of S/M as "Not a reproduction . . . of the structure of power" (*Homos* 88). My argument doesn't take up the specific question of the workings of power in, or the subversiveness of, S/M; my focus is on the potential for sex acts to shatter the liberal notion of the individual subject, a potential Bersani readily grants.

55. Butler, *Gender Trouble*, 97.

56. "Sade, sergent du sexe," *Cinématographe* 16 (December 1975–January 1976): 3–5, repr. in *Dits et écrits 1954–1988 par Michel Foucault*, ed. Daniel Defert and François Ewald, 4 vols. (Paris: Gallimard, 1994), 2: 821–22: "Il faut inventer avec le corps, avec ses éléments, ses surfaces, ses volumes, ses épaisseurs, un érotisme non disciplinaire: celui du corps à l'état volatil et diffus, avec ses rencontres de hasard et ses plaisirs sans calculs"; English translation modified from James Miller, *The Passion of Michel Foucault* (New York: Simon and Schuster, 1993), 278.

57. Quoted in David M. Halperin, *Saint Foucault: Towards a Gay Hagiography* (New York and Oxford: Oxford University Press, 1995), 94.

58. "[U]n erotisme . . . du corps à l'état . . . diffus"; "ce grand plaisir du corps en explosion": "Sade, sergent du sexe," 2:821–22; fragments quoted in translation by Miller, *Passion of Michel Foucault*, 278, 274.

59. Bob Gallagher and Alexander Wilson, "Sex, Power, and the Politics of Identity," *The Advocate*, 7 August 1984, 27, 30; according to Miller (*Passion of Michel Foucault*, 262–63) this interview took place in 1982. In the 1982 *Salmagundi* interview, Foucault linked courtly love with S/M, and made the same contrast as he does here.

60. See Saint Jerome, Letter 22, to Eustochium, which develops this idea in meticulous detail (sec. 5 et passim, in *Epistulae*, ed. Isidorus Hilberg, 3 vols., Corpus Scriptorum Ecclesiasticorum Latinorum 54–56 [Vienna: F. Tempsky, 1910–18], 1:143–211, esp. 149–50). Judith Butler, uncharacteristically on the side of the exegetes here, analyzes such a deconstruction in her *Bodies That Matter: On the Discursive Limits of "Sex"* (New York: Routledge, 1993), 244n7.

61. Douglas M. Moon, "The Role of Morgan la Fée in *Sir Gawain and the Green Knight*," *Neuphilologische Mitteilungen* 47 (1966): 31–57, esp. 33.

62. Borroff, *Sir Gawain*, 51.

63. Moon, "The Role of Morgan," 48.

64. H. Oskar Sommer, *The Vulgate Version of the Arthurian Romances*, 4:124; *Lancelot*, Part III, in *Lancelot-Grail: The Old French Arthurian Vulgate and Post-Vulgate in Translation*, 4 vols. to date, trans. Samuel N. Rosenberg (New York and London: Garland Publishing, 1993–), 2:313.

65. See Sheila Fisher, "Leaving Morgan Aside" and "Taken Men and Token Women." See also Gayle Margherita, *The Romance of Origins: Language and Sexual Difference in Middle English Literature* (Philadelphia: University of Pennsylvania Press, 1994), 129–51.

66. For the observation that male homosocial bonds are the operant power relations of romance see E. Jane Burns's Introduction to *Lancelot-Grail: The Old French Arthurian Vulgate and Post-Vulgate in Translation*, I:xxvi; Susan Crane, *Gender and Romance in Chaucer's* Canterbury Tales (Princeton: Princeton University Press, 1994); Roberta L. Krueger, "Love, Honor, and the Exchange of Women in *Yvain*: Some Remarks on the Female Reader," *Romance Notes* 25 (1985): 302–17; see also Christiane Marchello-Nizia, "Amour courtois, société masculine et figures du pouvoir," *Annales* 36 (1981): 969–82.

67. See Goldberg, *Sodometries*, 12.

68. Halperin, *Saint Foucault*, 15–16.

69. Heather Findlay, "Queer Dora: Hysteria, Sexual Politics, and Lacan's 'Intervention on Transference,'" *GLQ: A Journal of Lesbian and Gay Studies* 1 (1994): 323–47, esp. 336.

70. See Sarah Schulman, *My American History: Lesbian and Gay Life During the Reagan/Bush Years* (New York: Routledge, 1994), 216–217, 238.

71. "Sade, sergent du sexe" in *Dits et écrits*, 2:819: "Il y a là anarchisation du corps où les hiérarchies, les localisations et les dénominations, l'organicité, si vous voulez, sont en train de se défaire. . . . C'est une chose 'innommable,' 'inutilisable,' hors de tous les programmes du désir; c'est le corps rendu entièrement plastique par le plaisir: quelque chose qui s'ouvre, qui se tend, qui palpite, qui bat, qui bée." English translation modified from Miller, *Passion of Michel Foucault*, 274.

72. Hayden White, *The Content of the Form: Narrative Discourse and Historical Representation* (Baltimore and London: Johns Hopkins University Press, 1987), 104–41, at 105; noted in Halperin, *Saint Foucault*, 74.

73. Ed Cohen, "Foucauldian Necrologies: 'Gay' 'Politics'? Politically Gay?" *Textual Practice* 2.1 (Spring 1988), 87–101, at 96.

74. Biddy Martin, "Feminism, Criticism, and Foucault," *New German Critique* 27 (1982): 3–30, at 11.

75. Versions of this paper were presented at Western Washington University, the University of California, Santa Barbara, the University of Notre Dame, Bryn Mawr College, the International Medieval Congress at Western Michigan University, Kalamazoo, and the University of Southern California.

Index

Canterbury Tales (Chaucer), 82, 130
Capellanus, Andreas, 46
Carlson, David, 81
Carroz, Luiz, 87
Cassian, John (saint), 11, 12–13,
    14–16, 18
Cassiodorus, 27 n.13
Caxton, William, 79
Chance of the Dice, 102
Charley Varrick (film), 119
Chatwyn, William, 96
Chaucer, Geoffrey, 78, 79, 80, 82,
    84–85, 87, 89, 93, 97, 98
chivalric romance, 127, 136, 152
Cicero, 4, 5
Cistercian order, 1, 17
classical (Roman) education,
    memory of, 12–13, 14
Cleanness, 134
Cobain, Kurt, 117
Cohen, Ed, 155
compunctio cordis, 2, 19, 21, 22–23
compunctus (compunction), 2, 7, 21
concupiscentia, 37
confession, 37, 143, 144
Confessions (Augustine), 26 n.6
Conforte of Louers (Hawes), 79, 81–92,
    93, 109–10
contra naturam (against nature), 57,
    135, 136
Conuersyon of Swerers (Hawes), 83
conversio, 18
conversion, 18
converto, 20
Cooper, Dennis, 124
corporeality: in medieval (and
    Tudor) England, xii, xiv–xv,
    78–110; of rote material, 14.
    See also body
courtly love, 148
Cromwell, Oliver, 96
cura, 20
curiositas, 11, 12, 16, 17, 20
cursus curiae romanae, 42, 51
Curtius, Ernst Robert, xi

De amore (Capellanus), 46
de Bury, Richard (bishop of

Durham), 34–62 passim; death
    of, 61–62; episcopal seal of, 39,
    64; immortality of, 60–61; oak
    chest of, 39–40, 65
Deleuze, Gilles, 35
Deliverance (film), 121, 124
Denkmal, 61
Derrida, Jacques, 35
desexualization, 147
desire, xii, xiii–xiv, 34–62 passim.
    See also heterosexuality; homo-
    sexuality
Devonshire Manuscript (London,
    British Library, Add. 17492), 97,
    99
devotion. See desire
Dibdin, Thomas Frognall, 34
Didymus, 27 n.13
Dinshaw, Carolyn, 35
Discipline and Punish (Foucault), 138,
    147, 148
disorder, 11
dis-placement, 16–17
distraction (bad curiositas), 20

Eco, Umberto, 125, 126
Edward, Duke of Buckingham, 96
Edward III (king of England), 38
Elton, G. R., 96
emotional memories, 10, 21, 24–25
emotions, control of, 20
Enders, Jody, 3
Eneas: Roman du XIIe siècle, 127
engraving, 94, 97
Erasmus, Desiderius, 76–77 n.40, 87
Eulalia, martyrdom of, ix–x
eye metaphors, 46

fetishes: body as, 88; books as, xiii,
    36–46, 47, 60, 61
Findlay, Heather, 153
Fisher, Sheila, 131, 152
Flores Bernardi (Paris, Bibliothéque
    Mazarine, MS 753), 66
forgetting, 11, 12, 13, 17, 18–20
Foucault, Michel, xi, 44, 117,
    136–55
Fox, Alistair, 83–84

Fradenburg, Louise, 3
Freud, Sigmund, 61, 107–8

Galen, 5
gaze, 50, 52, 94, 130–31
Gender Trouble (Butler), 154
Geoffrey of Auxerre, 31 n.33
Geoffrey of Vinsauf, 12
Goldberg, Jonathan, 84, 129, 138
Gorleston Psalter, 57
Gower, John, 82, 101
Grammar, trope of, 47–48, 68
Green, André, 47
Greenblatt, Stephen, 80, 86
Grey-Fitzpayn Hours (Cambridge,
  Fitzwilliam Museum,
  MS 242), 70

Halperin, David M., 138, 153
Hawes, Stephen, 78, 79, 80–92, 93,
  94, 108
Heng, Geraldine, 108
Henry V (king of England), 81
Henry VII (king of England), 82, 83
Henry VIII (king of England), 80, 81,
  83, 86, 96
Herculine Barbin, 147
Heroides (Ovid), 100
heterosexuality, 127, 129–30, 134,
  152
History of Sexuality (Foucault), 136–55
  passim
Homer, 4
homoeroticism, xvi, 122, 127,
  128–30, 135–36, 152
homophobia, 124
homosexuality, 137–40
hooks, bell, 123, 124–25
house of memory, 46. *See also*
  locational memory
Hugh of St. Victor, 24
hunt metaphors, 50, 128, 133–34,
  135

illuminated manuscripts, 56–57, 59
images (*phantasiai*), 10, 13, 14, 20,
  21, 25
inscription, 97

intentio, 10, 20
inventio, meanings of, 8–9
invention, 8, 9, 25–26
inventory, 8–9

Jeanneret, Michel, 51
Jerome (saint), 4, 50, 67, 149
Jesus Christ, body as a parchment
  page, 4–5
John of Salisbury, 50
Joyfull Meditation, A (Hawes), 83

Krafft-Ebing, Richard von, 36
Kritzman, Lawrence, 88, 94

Lacan, Jacques, 61
Lancelot, 127, 130, 152
Lanval, Le Lai de, 127
Legend of Good Women (Chaucer), 98
Lewis, C. S., 80
libraries, 40, 44–45, 55, 61
Livre de l'Archiloge Sophie (Paris,
  Bibliothéque Nationale,
  MS fr. 24233), 68
locational memory, 8–9, 11–12, 13,
  24
"Long Charter" of Christ, 4–5
longing, xii. *See also* desire
looking, 47. *See also* eye metaphors;
  gaze
love, 46. *See also* courtly love; desire
Love, Courtney, 117
Luria, A. R., 16–17
luxuria, 37
Lydgate, John, 82, 92, 93, 102
Lyndsay, David, 106, 112 n.16

Madness and Civilization (Foucault), 141
manuscript painting. *See* illuminated
  manuscripts
Marot, Clément, 88
Marrou, Henri, 14
Martin, Biddy, 155
Mary Tudor, 83
Mason, H. A., 80
meditation, 5, 7, 9, 15, 16, 21, 25
meletein, 7, 17
memoria, 1, 2, 3, 9, 11, 17, 24, 25